D1492002

TELEPEN

IRISH WILD MAMMALS:

A GUIDE TO THE LITERATURE

J. S. Fairley

———

IRISH WILD MAMMALS:

A GUIDE TO THE LITERATURE

———

GALWAY

1972

© 1972 J. S. Fairley

Edition limited to 400 copies.

Printed and bound by Corrib Printers, Galway.

PREFACE

The majority of the work on the wild mammals of Ireland has been published in the form of small papers and notes which are widely scattered through a variety of periodicals. In addition, information is sometimes set down in books on related or more general topics. This guide has therefore been compiled in the hope that it will facilitate reference to the available literature.

I would emphasize that this is, in fact, a selected bibliography and is concerned primarily with original data on the extant wild mammals published in the hundred and fifty years between 1820 and 1970. However, some references outside this period, together with useful reviews of knowledge in this field, have been added. Domestic mammals, even those which have been feral for several generations, have not been considered and neither have forms which have been long extinct. Papers solely concerned with fossils or bones in cave or lake deposits or in kitchen middens have also been omitted, though not general works on the origin of the Irish mammal fauna. It seemed logical to deal only with printed books, journals, reports and pamphlets and not with newspapers or mimeographed documents. The former are obviously not only more reliable, but also more readily accessible. Nevertheless, I have found it necessary to include selected references from a number of periodicals technically classed as newspapers in the British Museum Catalogue, such as *The Field*.

It would have been pointless to attempt to include every publication concerning Irish mammals. Numerous books on British mammals, some of them of considerable importance, repeat what is effectively only a list of species in Ireland and brief descriptions of the Irish hare and stoat. There seemed to be little advantage in considering these. Furthermore there was nothing to be gained by including reviews, summaries or notices of books or papers or, indeed, requests for information unless they themselves contributed something original. I have almost completely ignored notices of exhibits. I have also largely avoided the subjects of traditional fox-hunting, coursing, otter-hunting, introductions of Irish mammals to other countries and oddities of no zoological interest.

Journal titles have been abbreviated as in the *World List of Scientific Periodicals*. (Fourth Edition) 1963-65. Unrecorded titles are abbreviated to conform. Explanatory notes are included with many entries to indicate their scope, especially major works or those with obscure titles. References marked with an asterisk contain little or no new data on Irish mammals.

Inevitably I will have omitted some relevant material, even though every effort has been made to make the work as comprehensive as possible. I would be grateful if readers would bring any such omissions to my attention.

J.S.F.

Department of Zoology,

University College, Galway.

ACKNOWLEDGMENTS

I would like to record my thanks to the librarians of the following institutions for their valuable co-operation: the Belfast Municipal Library; the British Museum; the Linenhall Library, Belfast; the National Library of Ireland; the Queen's University of Belfast; the Royal Irish Academy; Trinity College, Dublin; the Ulster Museum; University College, Galway and the Zoological Society of London. Dr. C. O'Riordan and Mr. D. Erwin kindly made available the library facilities of the Natural History Departments of, respectively, the National Museum of Ireland and the Ulster Museum.

I am most grateful to Dr. M. E. Mitchell for much useful discussion and to Mr. F. L. Clark for help in checking references and indices.

IRISH WILD MAMMALS:

A GUIDE TO THE LITERATURE

1 **Abbot, W. M., 1922.**
Squirrels in Co. Cork. *Ir. Nat.*, **31**: 83.

2 **Adams, A. L., 1880.**
On the recent and extinct Irish mammals. *Scient. Proc. R. Dubl. Soc.*, (n.s.) **2**: 45-86.

3 **Adams, A. L., 1883.**
Report on the history of the Irish fossil mammals. *Proc. R. Ir. Acad.*, (2) **3**: 89-100.

Adams, L. E., 1884. See No. 6.

4 **Adams, L. E., 1905.**
Remains of common mole in Ireland. *Ir. Nat.*, **14**: 72.
● In pellet of bird of prey.

5 **Adams, L. E., 1906.**
Some local names in Surrey. *Zoologist,* (4) **10**: 439.
● Note on nesting and local name of pigmy shrew in Ireland.

6 **Adams, L. E., 1909.**
Helix nemoralis eaten by rabbits. *J. Conch., Lond.*, **12**: 268. This is first noted in Adams, L. E., 1884. *The*

Collector's Manual of British Land and Freshwater Shells. Bell. London. However, Ireland is not mentioned.

7 **Adams, L. E., 1926.**
The lesser shrew. *Ir. Nat. J.,* **1**: 106. ● Correspondence on dead shrews.

8 ***Aflalo, F. G., 1898.**
A Sketch of the Natural History of the British Isles. Blackwood. London.

9 **Alcock, N. H., 1898.**
Daubenton's bat (*Vespertilio daubentoni,* Leisler) in Co. Wicklow. *Ir. Nat.,* **7**: 256.

10 **Alcock, N. H., 1898.**
The whiskered bat in Co. Dublin. *Ir. Nat.,* **7**: 272.

11 **Alcock, N. H., 1899.**
The natural history of Irish bats. *Ir. Nat.,* **8**: 29-36, 53-57, 169-174. ● A thorough account.

12 **Alcock, N. H., 1899.**
The long-eared bat in Co. Waterford. *Ir. Nat.,* **8**: 52.

13 **Alcock, N. H., 1899.**
Capture of live bats. *Ir. Nat.,* **8**: 165.

14 **Alcock, N. H. and Moffat, C. B., 1901.**
The natural history of Irish bats. *Ir. Nat.,* **10**: 241-251.

15 **Allen, F. A., 1909.**
The wolf in Scotland and Ireland. *Trans. Caradoc*

Severn Vall. Fld Club, **5**: 68-74. ● Numerous references to Irish wolves.

16 **Allingham, H., 1879.**

Ballyshannon: its History and Antiquities with some Account of the Surrounding Countryside. Montgomery. Londonderry. ● Includes a brief general account of local mammals including marine forms.

17 **Allman, D., 1946.**

Observations on damage by hares at Clonegal Forest. *Ir. For.,* **3**: 92.

18 **Anderson, K., 1905.**

On some bats of the genus *Rhinolophus,* with remarks on their mutual affinities, and descriptions of twenty-six new forms. *Proc. zool. Soc. Lond.,* (1905) (2): 75-145. ● Brief mention of Irish specimens.

19 **Andersen, K., 1906.**

Comment on: Note on the type specimen of the bat *Micronycteris microtis* Miller. *Ann. Mag. nat. Hist.,* (7) **18**: 372-373. ● Shrinkage of the ears of Irish pipistrelle bats in alcohol.

20 **Anderson, R. J., 1901.**

A note on a beaked whale. *Ir. Nat.,* **10**: 117-119.

21 **Andersen, R. J., 1903.**

Notes on a specimen of the pilot whale (*Globiocephalia melas*). *Rep. Br. Ass. Advmt Sci.,* (Belfast: 1902): 650-651.

22 **Anderson, R. J., 1904.**

The teeth of *Mesoplodon hectori. Ir. Nat.,* **13**: 126-127.

23 **Anderson, R. J.,** 1905.

Some notes on the Cetacea of the Irish Atlantic coast.
Int. Congr. Zool., (Berne: 1904) **6**: 703-711.

24 **Anderson, R. J.,** 1912.

A Large Cetacean (New?). Published privately. Galway. (Pamphlet. Marked "Leaves from the Bio. Lab. Univ. Coll. Galway, N.U.I."). ● No locality given but this was almost certainly in Ireland.

25 **Anderson, R. J.,** 1913.

Notes on the skull of a grampus & c. *Rep. Br. Ass. Advmt Sci.,* (Dundee: 1912): 502-503.

26 **Anderson, R. J.,** 1914.

Some notes on a specimen of *Tursiops tursio* killed in Galway Bay. *Int. Congr. Zool.,* (Monaco: 1913) **9**: 557-558.

27 **Anderson, R. J.,** 1914.

Note on the skull and teeth of *Tursiops. Rep. Br. Ass. Advmt Sci.,* (Birmingham: 1913): 532-533. ● No locality given but this was almost certainly in Ireland.

28 **Andrews, W.,** 1855, 1860.

Notes on the birds of the south-west coast, and on the occurrence of the great shearwater (*Puffinus major*). *Proc. Dubl. nat. Hist. Soc.,* (1860) **1**: 80-85. Also in *Nat. Hist. Rev.,* (Proceedings of the Societies section) (1855) **2**: 91-97. ● Records fox, rabbits and seals on islands.

29 **Andrews, W.,** 1867.

On *Ziphius sowerbyi* (*Mesoplodon sowerbiensis* Van Beneden). *Trans. R. Ir. Acad.,* **24**: 429-438.

30 **Andrews, W.,** 1870.
   On a cetacean new to Ireland. *J. R. Dubl. Soc.,* **5**: 162, 188-192.

31 **Andrews, W.,** 1870.
   Notice on the capture of *Ziphius sowerbyi. Proc. R. Ir. Acad.,* (2) **1**: 49.

32 **Anon,** 1868.
   Otters in the Shannon. *Field,* **31**: 482.

33 **Anon.,** 1893.
   The badger (*Meles taxus*) in Ireland. *Ir. Nat.,* **2**: 25.

34 **Anon.,** 1898.
   Seals in the River Lee at Cork. *Ir. Nat.,* **7**: 88.

35 **Anon.,** 1904.
   Large grampus in mackerel net. *Field,* **103**: 1000.

36 **Anon.,** 1905.
   Bottle-nosed dolphins in Dublin Bay. *Field,* **105**: 807.

37 **Anon.,** 1911.
   Whaling off Mayo. *Field,* **118**: 774.

38 **Anon.,** 1916.
   Absence of the polecat from Ireland. *Field,* **127**: 661.
   ● Some supposed records. See also No. 951.

39 **Anon.,** 1951.
   Whale exhibited in Belfast, 1845. *Bull. Belf. munic. Art Gall. Mus.,* **1**: 68-69.

40 **Anon., 1955.**
Myxomatosis in hares. *Vet. Rec.,* **67**: 455. ● Irish hare infected.

41 **'Aquarius', 1871.**
Adventure with a seal. *Field,* **38**: 406. ● Seal takes fishing bait.

42 **'Aquarius', 1896.**
Hares going to ground. *Field,* **87**: 185.

43 **Armstrong, E. A., 1923.**
The squirrel in Ireland. *Ir. Nat.* **32**: 50-51.

44 **Arnason, A. and Pantelouris, E. M., 1966.**
Serum esterases of *Apodemus sylvaticus* and *Mus musculus. Comp. Biochem. Physiol.,* **19**: 53-61. ● Irish wild *Apodemus* used.

45 **Arthur, D. R., 1963.**
British Ticks. Butterworths. London. ● Includes a few Irish records of ticks, some possibly from wild mammals.

46 **Atkinson, K., 1899.**
A large rat. *Field,* **94**: 791.

47 **Augustin, 655.**
Liber de Mirabilus Sanctae Scripturae. (Translation of relevant section in: Reeves, W., 1861. *Proc. R. Ir. Acad.,* **7**: 514-522). ● The earliest known list of Irish mammals.

48 **Baily, W., 1886.**
Rambles on the Irish Coast (Part 1.—Dublin to

Howth). Sealy, Bryers and Walker. Dublin. ● Includes a list of local mammals including marine forms.

49 **Ball, R., 1838.**
Remarks on the species of seals (Phocidae) inhabiting the Irish seas. *Trans. R. Ir. Acad.,* **18**: 89-98.

50 **Ball, R., 1841.**
The common otter. *Ir. Penny J.,* **1**: 141-143.

51 **Ball, R., 1841.**
The hedgehog. *Ir. Penny J.,* **1**: 166-167.

52 **Ball, R., 1841.**
The common badger. *Ir. Penny J.,* **1**: 373-374.

53 **Ball, V., 1885.**
On the collection of the fossil Mammalia of Ireland in the science and art museum, Dublin. *Scient. Proc. R. Dubl. Soc.,* (n.s.) **3**: 333-348.

54 **Barclay, E. N., 1932.**
The introduction and extermination of roe deer in Ireland. *Nat. Hist. Mag.,* **3**: 265-267.

55 **Baring, C., 1907.**
Contributions to the natural history of Lambay. Mammals. *Ir. Nat.,* **16**: 19-23.

56 **Baring, C., 1915.**
Notes on the fauna and flora of Lambay. *Ir. Nat.,* **24**: 68-71.

57 **Baring, C., 1920.**
Note on the fauna of Lambay. *Ir. Nat.,* **29**: 69-70.

58 **Barlow, J. A., 1906.**
Pilot whale in Belfast Lough. *Field,* **108**: 991.

59 **Barrett-Hamilton, G. E. H., 1887.**
Black rat in Wexford. *Zoologist,* (3) **11**: 425.

60 **Barrett-Hamilton, G. E. H., 1888.**
Jay in Co. Wexford. *Zoologist,* (3) **12**: 67. ● Introduction of red squirrels.

61 **Barrett-Hamilton, G. E. H., 1888.**
Hybrid rats. *Zoologist,* (3) **12**: 141-142.

62 **Barrett-Hamilton, G. E. H., 1890.**
Bottle-nosed whale in Wexford and Wicklow. *Zoologist,* (3) **14**: 72.

63 **Barrett-Hamilton, G. E. H., 1890.**
Sperm whale in Mayo. *Zoologist,* (3) **14**: 72.

64 **Barrett-Hamilton, G. E. H., 1890.**
The white-sided dolphin in Ireland. *Zoologist,* (3) **14**: 384.

65 **Barrett-Hamilton, G. E. H., 1891.**
Leaping powers of the Irish hare (*Lepus variabilis*). *Zoologist,* (3) **15**: 60-61.

66 **Barrett-Hamilton, G. E. H., 1891.**
Sibbald's rorqual on the Irish coast. *Zoologist,* (3) **15**: 306-308.

67 **Barrett-Hamilton, G. E. H., 1892.**
Breeding habits of the otter (*Lutra vulgaris*) and the

squirrel (*Sciurus vulgaris*). *Ir. Nat.*, **1**: 127. ● Largely a request for information.

68 **Barrett-Hamilton, G. E. H.,** 1892.
Mus alexandrinus in Ireland. *Zoologist,* (3) **16**: 75.

69 **Barrett-Hamilton, G. E. H.,** 1892.
Lesser rorqual in Kerry. *Zoologist,* (3) **16**: 75.

70 **Barrett-Hamilton, G. E. H.,** 1892.
Young squirrels. *Zoologist,* (3) **16**: 328.

71 **Barrett-Hamilton, G. E. H.,** 1894.
The rabbit on the Irish islands. *Ir. Nat.*, **3**: 68.
● Three records.

72 **Barrett-Hamilton, G. E. H.,** 1895.
Irish mammals. *Ir. Nat.*, **4**: 65-72, 85-92, 167. ● Largely a review of No. 535 but with some original information.

73 **Barrett-Hamilton, G. E. H.,** 1895.
Irish hare turning white in winter. *Zoologist,* (3) **19**: 185-186.

74 **Barrett-Hamilton, G. E. H.,** 1896.
Irish hare going to ground. *Ir. Nat.*, **5**: 119.

75 **Barrett-Hamilton, G. E. H.,** 1898.
Notes on the introduction of the brown hare into Ireland. *Ir. Nat.*, **7**: 69-76. ● A detailed list of introductions.

76 **Barrett-Hamilton, G. E. H.,** 1898.
Introduction of Scotch hares in Ireland and south Scotland. *Ir. Nat.*, **7**: 76.

77 **Barrett-Hamilton, G. E. H.,** 1899.
Lesser rorqual on the coast of Cork. *Ir. Nat.,* **8**: 27.

78 **Barrett-Hamilton, G. E. H.,** 1899.
Supposed occurrence of lesser rorqual in the Swilly. *Ir. Nat.,* **8**: 210. ● Criticism of No. 399.

79 **Barrett-Hamilton, G. E. H.,** 1899.
Exhibition of, and remarks upon, a skin of the varying hare (*Lepus variabilis*) in the spring moulting stage. *Proc. zool. Soc. Lond.,* (1899): 598-599. ● Includes a brief note on winter whitening in Irish hares.

80 **Barrett-Hamilton, G. E. H.,** 1900.
New locality for Leisler's bat. *Ir. Nat.,* **9**: 134.

81 **Barrett-Hamilton, G. E. H.,** 1900.
Exhibition of skins of the variable hare (*Lepus timidus* Linn.) showing colour-variations, and descriptions of sub-species and varieties of this species. *Proc. zool. Soc. Lond.,* (1900): 87-92.

82 **Barrett-Hamilton, G. E. H.,** 1900.
On the geographical and individual variation in *Mus sylvaticus* and its allies. *Proc. zool. Soc. Lond.,* (1900): 387-428.

83 **Barrett-Hamilton, G. E. H.,** 1901.
Irish hare entering a burrow. *Ir. Nat.,* **10**: 73.

84 **Barrett-Hamilton, G. E. H.,** 1901.
Probable occurrence of the lesser rorqual on the coast of Co. Wexford. *Ir. Nat.,* **10**: 74.

85   **Barrett-Hamilton, G. E. H., 1901.**
The colouration of the variable hare. *Zoologist,* (4)
5: 221-222. ● A white hare in April.

86   **Barrett-Hamilton, G. E. H., 1903.**
Live marten in Co. Wexford. *Ir. Nat.,* **12**: 320.

87   **Barrett-Hamilton, G. E. H., 1908.**
Whiskered bat in Co. Wexford. *Ir. Nat.,* **17**: 207.

88   **Barrett-Hamilton, G. E. H., 1909.**
Number of young of stoat. *Ir. Nat.,* **18**: 208.

89   **Barrett-Hamilton, G. E. H., 1909.**
The Irish otter. *Ir. Nat.,* **18**: 208.

90   **Barrett-Hamilton, G. E. H., 1910.**
The American facies of the British and Irish fauna.
Ir. Nat., **19**: 12.

91   **Barrett-Hamilton, G. E. H., 1911.**
Former occurrence of the wild cat in Ireland. *Ir.
Nat.,* **20**: 55.

92   **Barrett-Hamilton, G. E. H., 1912.**
The weight of Irish hares. *Ir. Nat.,* **21**: 234.

93   **Barrett-Hamilton, G. E. H., 1912.**
Mammalia. Clare Island Survey. Part 17. Section ii.
Proc. R. Ir. Acad., **31**: 1-14.

94   **Barrett-Hamilton, G. E. H., 1913.**
Daubenton's bat in County Waterford. *Ir. Nat.,* **22**:
63.

95   Barrett-Hamilton, G. E. H. and Hinton, M. A. C., 1910-21.
A History of British Mammals. Gurney and Jackson.
London. ● A thorough account of the Irish mammals
except the Artiodactyla, Carnivora and Cetacea.

96   Barrett-Hamilton, G. E. H. and Patterson, R., 1894.
The marten in Ireland. *Zoologist,* (3) **18**: 134-142,
187. ● An informative account.

97   Barrington, E. C., 1893.
Hairy-armed bat (*Vesperugo leisleri*) in Co. Dublin.
Ir. Nat., **2**: 277.

98   Barrington, E. C., 1893.
Hairy-armed bat in Co. Dublin. *Zoologist,* (3) **17**:
426-427. ● This is practically identical to the last
reference.

99   Barrington, J. S., 1926.
Increase of the badger. *Ir. Nat. J.,* **1**: 168.

100   Barrington, R. M., 1867.
Rats eating grapes. *Zoologist,* (2) **2**: 987.

101   Barrington, R. M., 1869.
Abnormal dentition in the rabbit. *Zoologist,* (2) **4**:
1843.

102   Barrington, R. M., 1874.
The hairy-armed bat (*Scotophilus leisleri*) in Ireland. *Zoologist,* (2) **9**: 4071-4074.

103   Barrington, R. M., 1874, 1875.
A new bat-tick. *Proc. Dubl. microsc. Club,* (1874) **3**:
27. Also in *Q. Jl microsc. Sci.,* (1875) (2) **15**: 104.

104 **Barrington, R. M., 1875.**
Hairy-armed bat in the County Wicklow. *Zoologist,* (2) **10**: 4532.

105 **Barrington, R. M., 1875.**
Mouse eating flies. *Zoologist,* (2) **10**: 4571-5472. ● In captivity.

106 **Barrington, R. M., 1875.**
Rat killing its own species. *Zoologist,* (2) **10**: 4663-4664.

107 **Barrington, R. M., 1877.**
The natural history of Donegal. *Zoologist,* (3) **1**: 223.

108 **Barrington, R. M., (in McAlister, A. and M'Nabb, W. R. [eds.]), 1878.**
Guide to the County of Dublin. Hodges, Foster and Figgis. Dublin. ● Note on the mammals. (For British Association meeting in Dublin).

109 **Barrington, R. M., 1878.**
Difference in mode of attacking turnips by rabbits and rats. *Zoologist,* (3) **2**: 178.

110 **Barrington, R. M., 1880.**
On the introduction of the squirrel into Ireland. *Scient. Proc. R. Dubl. Soc.,* (n.s.) **2**: 615-631. ● A comprehensive list of the known introductions of the red squirrel.

111 **Barrington, R. M., 1882.**
On the breeding habits of the long-tailed field mouse. *Zoologist,* (3) **6**: 121-123. ● In captivity.

112 **Barrington, R. M.,** 1883.
Hairy-armed bat in Co. Fermanagh. *Zoologist,* (3) **7**: 116.

113 **Barrington, R. M.,** 1885.
Attempted acclimatisation of the dormouse in Ireland. *Zoologist,* (3) **9**: 479. ● Introduction.

114 **Barrington, R. M.,** 1900.
The Migration of Birds as Observed at Irish Lighthouses and Lightships. Porter. London. ● Includes records of bats.

115 **Barrington, R. M.,** 1909.
Do rabbits eat *Arum maculatum? Ir. Nat.,* **18**: 157.

116 **Barrington, R. M.,** 1910.
Measurements of martens. *Ir. Nat.,* **19**: 104.

117 **Barrington, R. M.,** 1913.
The Irish wild cat. *Ir. Nat.,* **22**: 124.

118 **Barrington, R. M.,** 1915.
Decrease of the squirrel. *Ir. Nat.,* **24**: 42.

119 **Bayly, H. L.,** 1894.
The marten in Co. Wicklow. *Zoologist,* (3) **18**: 394-395.

120 **B.C.E.,** 1950.
Pine marten and polecat. *Field,* **196**: 1137.

121 **Beirne, B. P.,** 1947.
The history of British land mammals. *Ann. Mag. nat. Hist.,* (11) **14**: 501-514.

122 **Beirne, B. P.,** 1948.
Notes on the history of the British and Irish bats. *Ir. Nat. J.,* **9**: 153-155. ● Post-glacial colonization of Ireland by bats.

123 **Beirne, B. P.,** 1952.
The Origin and History of the British Fauna. Methuen. London.

124 **Belfast Naturalist's Field Club,** 1874.
Guide to Belfast and the Adjacent Counties. Belfast Naturalist's Field Club. Belfast. ● Notes on mammals including a little new information. (For British Association meeting in Belfast).

125 **Belfast Naturalist's Field Club,** 1902.
A Guide to Belfast and the Counties of Down and Antrim. Belfast Naturalist's Field Club. Belfast. ● Notes on mammals including a little new information. Record of bat bug, also given in Halbert, J. N., 1935. *Proc. R. Ir. Acad.,* 42B: 221-318. (For British Association meeting in Belfast).

126 **Bell, T.,** 1837 (1874).
A History of British Quadrupeds Including the Cetacea. Van Voorst. London. (Second edition 1874).

127 **Bellingham, O'B.,** 1840.
Catalogue of the Entozoa indigenous to Ireland; with observations. *Mag. nat. Hist.,* (2) **4**: 343-351.

128 **Bellingham, O'B.,** 1843.
Short description of a bottle-nosed whale stranded upon the coast of Co. Louth. *Ann. Mag. nat. Hist.,* **11**: 414-415.

129 **Bellingham, O'B.,** 1844.
Catalogue of Irish Entozoa, with observations. *Ann. Mag. nat. Hist.,* **13**: 101-105, 167-174, 254-260, 335-340, 422-430. **14**: 162-165, 251-256, 317-323, 396-403, 471-479.

130 **Bentley, E. W.,** 1959.
The distribution and status of *Rattus rattus* L. in the United Kingdom in 1951 and 1956. *J. Anim. Ecol.,* **28**: 299-308.

131 **Bentley, E. W.,** 1964.
A further loss of ground by *Rattus rattus* L. in the United Kingdom during 1956-61. *J. Anim. Ecol.,* **33**: 371-373.

132 **Berry, R. J.,** 1969.
History in the evolution of *Apodemus sylvaticus* (Mammalia) at one edge of its range. *J. Zool., Lond.,* **159**: 311-328. ● Epigenetic features in Irish mice.

133 **Bingley, W.,** 1809.
Memoirs of British Quadrupeds. Darton and Harvey. London. ● A few brief references.

Boate, G., Molyneux, T. et al. 1755. See No. 620.

134 **Borrer, W.,** 1877.
Occurrence of the weasel in Ireland. *Zoologist,* (3) **1**: 291.

135 **Boyle, C. L.,** 1954.
Red deer in Ireland *Oryx,* **2**: 394-395.

136 **Brenan, S. A.,** 1897.
A plague of rats at Cushendun. *Ir. Nat.,* **6**: 60.

137   **Brenan, S. A.,** 1898.
      The harvest mouse. *Ir. Nat.,* **7**: 125. ● Supposed record.

138   **Brooke, A. B.,** 1870.
      Natural history of Wicklow and Kerry. *Zoologist,* (2) **5**: 2281-2285. ● Only Carnivora mentioned.

139   **Brooke, D.,** 1889.
      Deer rutting in January. *Field,* **73**: 126.

140   **Brooke, D.,** 1895.
      Abnormal dentition in red-deer. *Field,* **86**: 523.

141   **Brooke, D.,** 1898.
      Hybrid red deer. *Field,* **92**: 182.

142   **Brown, J. J., Kersley, L. W. and McDonald, R.,** 1951.
      Notes on the flora and fauna of the Maidens. *Ir. Nat. J.,* **10**: 208-211. ● Brown rat and seals recorded.

143   **Browne, C. R.,** 1894.
      The ethnography of Inishboffin and Inishark, County Galway. *Proc. R. Ir. Acad,* (3) **3**: 317-370. ● Rabbits. Mentions otters, porpoises and seals around coasts.

144   **Brunker, J. P.,** 1951.
      Rats eating hawthorn berries. *Ir. Nat. J.,* **10**: 137.

145   **Brunton, T.,** 1874.
      Birds observed at Glenarm Castle. *Zoologist,* (2) **9**: 3829-3830. ● Rabbit remains in gut of buzzard.

146   **Burfield, S. T.,** 1912.
      Belmullet whaling station. Report of the committee.

Rep. Br. Ass. Advmt Sci., (Portsmouth: 1911): 121-125. ● A detailed report of several aspects of the whales and whale-fishing.

147   Burfield, S. T., 1913.
Belmullet whaling station. Report of the committee. *Rep. Br. Ass. Advmt Sci.,* (Dundee: 1912): 145-186. ● A comprehensive report covering many aspects of the whales and whale-fishing.

148   Butler, E. A., 1891.
White curlew and marten in Co. Down. *Field,* **78**: 88. ● Not a white marten.

149   C., 1886.
Badger and foxes in one earth. *Field,* **67**: 640. ● Heresay.

150   Cabot, D., 1962.
The pigmy or lesser shrew. (*Sorex minutus* L.) on Tory Island, Co. Donegal. *Ir. Nat. J.,* **14**: 82.

151   Cabot, D., 1965.
Cuvier's whale *Ziphius cavirostris,* on Achill Island, Co. Mayo. *Ir. Nat. J.,* **15**: 72-73.

152   Cabot, D., 1966.
A further example of Cuvier's whale *Ziphius cavirostris* from the west coast of Ireland. *Ir. Nat. J.,* **15**: 212.

153   Cabot, D., 1967.
A sperm whale, *Physeter catodon* (L.) on Achill Island, Co. Mayo, March 1967. *Ir. Nat. J.,* **15**: 326.

154 **Cabot, D., 1969.**
The pigmy or lesser shrew, *Sorex minutus* L., on Inis-kea South, Co. Mayo. *Ir. Nat. J.,* **16**: 243.

155 **Campbell, D. C., 1907.**
Humpbacked whale at Moville, Lough Foyle. *Ir. Nat.,* **16**: 352.

156 **Carlisle, R. W., Palmer, R. F. and Skillen, S., 1960.**
Natterer's bat, *Myotis nattereri* Kuhl., Castlecoole, Co. Fermanagh. *Ir. Nat. J.,* **13**: 121. ● Nycteribiid parasite also found.

157 **Carlisle, R. W. and Skillen, S., 1960.**
Parasites on Irish bats. *Ir. Nat. J.,* **13**: 168-169. ● Flea, mites.

158 **Carlisle, R. W. and Skillen, S., 1960.**
Fleas from Irish bats. *Ir. Nat. J.,* **13**: 185-186.

159 **Carpenter, G. H., 1902.**
Whiskered bat in Co. Wexford. *Ir. Nat.,* **11**: 103.

160 **Carr, D., 1902.**
The weight of red deer. *Field,* **100**: 688.

161 **Carte, A. and McAlister, A., 1868.**
On the anatomy of *Balaenoptera rostrata*. *Phil. Trans. R. Soc.,* **158**: 201-261.

162 **Catford, B. B., 1930.**
A friendly baby seal. *Ir. Nat. J.,* **3**: 90.

163 **C. E. B., 1918.**
Pine marten in Co. Clare. *Field,* **132**: 414.

164 **Chase, C. D., 1948.**
The Natural History of Campbell College and Cabin Hill, Belfast. Published privately. Belfast. ● Includes notes on the mammals.

165 **C. J. R., 1893.**
Hare breaking its back. *Field*, **82**: 673.

166 **Claassens, A. J. M., 1965.**
Fleas from the woodmouse *Apodemus sylvaticus sylvaticus* (L.) in Co. Cork. *Entomologist's Gaz.*, **16**: 95-104.

167 **Claassens, A. J. M., 1965.**
Leptinus testaceus Müller (Col., Silphidae), new records. *Ir. Nat. J.*, **15**: 60-62. ● Specimens from small mammals.

168 **Claassens, A. J. M. and O'Gorman, F., 1965.**
The bank vole *Clethrionomys glareolus* Schreber: a mammal new to Ireland. *Nature, Lond.*, **205**: 923-924.

169 **Claassens, A. J. M. and O'Rourke, F. J., 1964.**
Leptinus testaceus Müll. (Col. Silphidae) a possibly parasitic beetle new to Co. Cork. *Entomologist's Gaz.*, **15**: 49-50. ● From fieldmouse.

170 **Claassens, A. J. M. and O'Rourke, F. J., 1966.**
The distribution and general ecology of the Irish Siphonaptera. *Proc. R. Ir. Acad.*, **64B**: 413-463. ● Includes all previous records to 1962 and many new ones.

171 **Clark, F. L., 1971.**
The common lizard, *Lacerta vivipera* Jacquin, and

the pygmy shrew, *Sorex minutus* L., on Inishmore, Aran Islands, Co. Galway. *Ir. Nat. J.,* **17**: 24.

172 **Clark, F. L. and Fairley, J. S.,** 1971.
Helminths from Irish small mammals. *Vet. Rec.,* **88**: 523.

173 **Clark, W. E. and Barrett-Hamilton, G. E. H.,** 1891.
On the identity and distribution of the Irish rat, *Mus hibernicus* Thompson. *Zoologist,* (3) **15**: 1-9.

174 **Clarke, W. E. and Barrett-Hamilton, G. E. H.,** 1891.
Melanism in mammals and the Irish rat. *Zoologist,* (3) **15**: 59-60.

175 **'Cleenish',** 1891.
Irish and English hares. *Field,* **78**: 546. ● Introduction of English hares which later died out.

176 ***Clermont, Lord,** 1859.
Quadrupeds and reptiles of Europe. Van Voorst. London. ● A few references to Ireland.

177 **Clermont, Lord,** 1882.
Change of colour in the Irish hare. *Zoologist,* (3) **6**: 107-108.

178 **Clowes, E. F.,** 1933.
Stoat feeding young on rock pipits. *Ir. Nat. J.,* **4**: 217-218.

179 **Coates, A. E.,** 1889.
Hares going to ground. *Field,* **74**: 418.

180 **Cocks, A. H.,** 1897.
Pine marten in Ireland. *Zoologist,* (4) **1**: 269-270.

181 **Coghill, H. E.,** 1909.
Mice devouring snails. *Ir. Nat.,* **18**: 27.

182 **Colby, T.,** 1837.
Ordnance Survey of the County of Londonderry. Vol. 1. Memoir of the City and North Western Liberties. Parish of Templemore. Hodges and Smith. Dublin. ● Records a colony of long-eared bats, and otters.

183 **Colgan, N.,** 1911.
Gaelic plant and animal names and associated folklore. Clare Island Survey. Part 4. *Proc. R. Ir. Acad.,* **31**: 1-30.

184 **Collett, R.,** 1909.
A few notes on the whale *Balaena glacialis* and its capture in recent years in the north Atlantic by Norwegian whalers. *Proc. zool. Soc. Lond.,* (1909): 91-98. ● Records of two whales from Ireland.

185 **Collins, A. J.,** 1892-83.
Hybrid between hare and rabbit (*Lepus variabilis* and *L. cuniculus*). *Ir. Nat.,* **1**: 147. **2**: 25. ● In fact an 'English' hare (species uncertain).

186 **Collins, J. J.,** 1955.
Myxomatosis in the common hare—*Lepus europaeus* —II. *Ir. vet. J.,* **9**: 268-269. ● Hare as a possible carrier of myxomatosis. (*L. europaeus?*). See also No. 940.

187 **Corbet, G. B.,** 1961.
Origin of the British insular races of the small mammals and of the Lusitanean fauna. *Nature, Lond.,* **191**: 1037-1047.

188 **Corbet, G. B.,** 1971.
Provisional distribution maps of British mammals. *Mammal Rev.*, **1**: 95-142. ● Considerable information for Ireland.

189 **Corbett, J.,** 1963.
The last wolf in Britain. *Cntry Life,* **133**: 1327.

190 **Cork, D., Cowlin, R. A. D. and Page, W. W.,** 1969.
Notes on the distribution and abundance of small mammals in south-west Ireland. *J. Zool., Lond.,* **158**: 216-221. ● Includes ectoparasites: fleas, mites, ticks.

191 **Corridan, J. P. and Gray, J. J.,** 1969.
Trichinosis in south-west Ireland. *Br. Med. J.,* (1969) (2): 727-730. ● An outbreak described and the possible rôle of wild carnivores discussed.

192 **Corridan, J. P., O'Rourke, F. J. and Verling, M.,** 1969.
Trichinella spiralis in the red fox (*Vulpes vulpes*) in Ireland. *Nature, Lond.,* **222**: 1191.

193 **Cox, H.,** 1906.
Hares swimming. *Field,* **108**: 540.

194 **Crawford, G. B.,** 1915.
Black rat in Dublin. *Ir. Nat.,* **24**: 75.

195 **Creaghe-Haward, L. C.,** 1903.
Marten in Co. Kerry. *Field,* **102**: 1001.

196 **C.R.G.,** 1885.
The weasel in Ireland. *Field,* **66**: 785. ● Weasel carries dead weasel. (In fact stoats).

197 **Crouch, W.,** 1891.
Sibbald's rorqual on the Irish coast. *Zoologist,* (3) **15**: 215.

198 **Cunningham, L. M.,** 1952.
Melanistic squirrels. *Cntry Life,* **111**: 363.

Cusack, M. F., 1875. See No. 415.

199 **Dadd, M. N.,** 1970.
Overlap of variation in British and European mammal populations. *Symp. zool. Soc. Lond.,* **26**: 117-125. ● Irish stoats and otters.

200 **D'Alton, J.,** 1838.
The History of the County of Dublin. Hodges and Smith. Dublin. ● Very little. Brief note on deer and a few distributional records.

201 **Daly, D.,** 1897.
Albino shrew in Co. Limerick. *Field,* **90**: 318.

202 **Daniel, R. J. and Hamilton, J. E.,** 1914.
Belmullet whaling station. Interim report of the committee. *Rep. Br. Ass. Advmt Sci.,* (Birmingham: 1913): 154-155.

203 **D'Arcy-Irvine, C. C.,** 1910.
The marten in Co. Fermanagh. *Field,* **116**: 779.

204 **Darling, J. F.,** 1883.
A black and white stoat. *Field,* **61**: 431.

205 **Darling J. F.,** 1883.
Marten in Co. Clare. *Zoologist,* (3) **7**: 252.

206 **Darling, J. F.,** 1883.
Natterer's bat in Co. Cork. *Zoologist,* (3) **7**: 294-295.

207 **Darling, J. F.,** 1916.
Some notes on otters. *Ir. Nat.,* **25**: 67-68.

208 **Davies, E.,** 1874.
Irish hare turning white in winter. *Field,* **44**: 31.

209 **Davies, J. L.,** 1957.
The geography of the grey seal. *J. Mammal.,* **38**: 297-316.

210 **Davis, R.,** 1846.
Carnivorous propensity of hedgehogs. *Zoologist,* **4**: 1293-1294. ● Rabbit eaten.

211 **Day, J. W.,** 1938.
The Dog in Sport. Harrap. London. ● Deer. Narrative.

212 **Day, M. G.,** 1968.
Food habits of British stoats and weasels. *J. Zool., Lond.,* **155**: 485-497. ● Some Irish stoats included (number unspecified) but they are not distinguished from British material in results.

213 **Deane, C. D.,** 1948.
Lesser rorqual stranded on coast of County Antrim. *Ir. Nat. J.,* **9**: 123.

214 **Deane, C. D.,** 1950.
The fox in Northern Ireland. *Ir. Nat. J.,* **10**: 93-94. ● Speculation on the causes of an increase in foxes. Bounty figures.

215 **Deane, C. D.,** 1951.
Hare breeding beneath a hut. *Ir. Nat. J.,* **10**: 197.

216 **Deane, C. D.,** 1952.
The 'black' rat in the north of Ireland. *Ir. Nat. J.,* **10**: 296-298.

217 **Deane, C. D.,** 1952.
Pine martens in counties Tyrone and Down. *Ir. Nat. J.,* **10**: 303.

218 **Deane, C. D.,** 1955.
Note on myxomatosis in hares. *Bull. Mammal Soc. Br. Isles,* **3**: 20. ● Includes a brief account of the spread of myxomatosis in Ireland.

219 **Deane, C. D.,** 1962.
Irish golden eagles and a link with Scotland. *Br. Birds,* **55**: 272-274. ● Prey: hares and rabbits, the former from Scotland.

220 ***Deane, C. D.,** 1964.
Introduced mammals in Ireland. *Bull. Mammal Soc. Br. Isles,* **21**: 2. ● A concise and yet highly informative account.

221 **Deane, C. D. and O'Gorman, F.,** 1969.
The spread of feral mink in Ireland. *Ir. Nat. J.,* **16**: 198-202. ● Numerous records and data on escapes from mink farms.

222 **De Barry, R. S.,** 1874.
Maternal instincts of a stoat. *Field,* **43**: 545.

223 **Delap, M. J.,** 1904.
Seal caught on a handline. *Ir. Nat.,* **13**: 49.

224 **Delap, P.,** 1936.
Deer in Wicklow. *Ir. Nat. J.,* **6**: 82-88.

225 **Delap, P.,** 1957.
Some notes on the social habits of the British deer. *Proc. zool. Soc. Lond.,* **128**: 608-612.

226 **Dennehy, T. J.,** 1905.
A black hare in Co. Kerry. *Field,* **105**: 905.

227 **Dent, H. C.,** 1890.
Hares swimming. *Field,* **75**: 892.

228 **Department of Education (Republic of Ireland),** 1927-38.
Rep. natn. Mus. Ire., (1927-38). ● Contain details of additions to the National Museum of Ireland (Dublin) collections including many mammal specimens, often with provenance. Earlier and later years of virtually no interest in this respect.

229 **Derg, Lord,** 1887.
Stoats and rabbits. *Field,* **69**: 29. ● Stoat playing?

230 **Derg, Lord,** 1887.
The squirrel in Co. Tipperary. *Field,* **70**: 969.

231 **Derg, Lord,** 1888.
Otters attacking a dog. *Field,* **71**: 192. ● Heresay.

232 **Dickie, G.,** 1858, 1859.
On the teeth of *Hyperoodon. Proc. Dubl. Univ. zool. bot. Ass.,* (1859) **1**: 6. Also in *Nat. Hist. Rev.,* (Proceedings of the Societies section) (1858) **5**: 50-51.

233 **Digby, R.,** 1893.
Cats catching squirrels. *Field,* **82**: 714.

234 **Dillon, R. E., 1906.**
Bat taking a trout fly. *Ir. Nat. J.,* **15**: 278.

235 **Donovan, E., Hayes, R., O'Donovan, J. and Cunneen, M., 1967.**
Doubling of the renal vessels of the rabbit. *Ir. Nat. J.,* **15**: 326-327.

236 **Douthwaite, R. J., 1966.**
Cambridge Irish seabird project: mammals. *Camb. Exped. J.,* **2**: 32-35. ● Mammals on and around islands in the south-west. Ectoparasites.

237 **Dover, W. K., 1877.**
Absence of the weasel from Ireland. *Zoologist,* (3) **1**: 440.

238 **Dowling, J. J., 1894.**
Marten in Co. Dublin. *Zoologist,* (3) **18**: 149-150.

239 **'Dublin', 1882.**
The habits of hedgehogs. *Field,* **60**: 891.

240 **Dublin Natural History Society, 1854.**
(Records of squirrels and fieldmice). *Proc. Dubl. nat. Hist. Soc.,* in *Nat. Hist. Rev.,* (Proceedings of the Societies section) **1**: 26.

241 **Dunscombe, R., 1881.**
Otter seizing prey while hunted. *Field,* **58**: 153.

242 **E., 1896.**
Weights of wild rabbit. *Field,* **88**: 814. ● A very large rabbit.

243 **Edwards, D. J. W.,** 1899.
A fox's larder. *Field,* **93**: 765. ● Animal remains in earth (including a stoat).

244 **E.I.G.,** 1908.
Otters in Co. Kildare. *Field,* **112**: 627.

245 **Ellison, A.,** 1888.
Squirrels robbing birds' nests. *Zoologist,* (3) **12**: 105.

246 **'Extraneous',** 1875.
Marten cat in the County of Sligo. *Field,* **45**: 16. ● Heresay record.

247 **Eyton, T.,** 1838.
Irish hare (*Lepus hibernicus,* Yarrell). *Mag. Zool. Bot.,* **2**: 283-284. ● Comparison of skeletons of Irish and brown hares.

248 **Fahie, C. J.,** 1887.
Rabbit taking to the water. *Field,* **70**: 486.

249 **Fairley, J. S.,** 1963.
Doratopsylla dasycnema, a flea previously unrecorded in Ireland. *Ir. Nat. J.,* **14**: 22. ● From fieldmouse.

250 **Fairley, J. S.,** 1963.
Fleas from the fieldmouse *Apodemus sylvaticus* (L.) in Co. Down. *Ir. Nat. J.,* **14**: 145-149.

251 **Fairley, J. S.,** 1963.
Mesostigmatid mites from the fieldmouse in Co. Down and a note on the beetle *Leptinus testaceus* Müll. *Ir. Nat. J.,* **14**: 165-167.

252 **Fairley, J. S.,** 1964.
A collection of fieldmice from Rathlin Island, Northern Ireland. *Ann. Mag. nat. Hist.,* (13) **7**: 27-31.
● A large insular race of fieldmouse. Other mammals recorded. Ectoparasites.

253 **Fairley, J. S.,** 1964.
The fieldmouse on some Irish islands. *Ir. Nat. J.,* **14**: 309-311. Ectoparasites.

254 **Fairley, J. S.,** 1965.
The food of the fox *Vulpes vulpes* (L.) in Co. Down. *Ir. Nat. J.,* **15**: 2-5.

255 **Fairley, J. S.,** 1965.
Further observations on the distribution of the epifauna of the fieldmouse (*Apodemus sylvaticus* [L.]) in Ireland. *Ir. Nat. J.,* **15**: 67-69.

256 **Fairley, J. S.,** 1965.
Fieldmice at high altitude in Co. Kerry, Ireland. *Proc. zool., Soc. Lond.,* **145**: 144-145. ● A shrew was also taken.

257 **Fairley, J. S.,** 1966.
An indication of the food of the short-eared owl in Ireland. *Br. Birds,* **59**: 307-308. ● From analyses of pellets.

258 **Fairley, J. S.,** 1966.
Analyses of barn owl pellets at an Irish roost. *Br. Birds,* **59**: 338-340.

259 **Fairley, J. S.,** 1966.
An indication of the food of the fox in Northern Ire-

land after myxomatosis. *Ir. Nat. J.*, **15**: 149-151. ● Analyses of stomach contents and faeces.

260 **Fairley, J. S., 1967.**
Food of long-eared owls in north-east Ireland. *Br. Birds*, **60**: 130-135. ● From analyses of pellets.

261 **Fairley, J. S., 1967.**
The food of foxes in north-east Ireland. *Bull. Mammal Soc. Br. Isles*, **28**: 3-4. ● All data incorporated in No. 284.

262 **Fairley, J. S., 1967.**
An indication of the food of the badger in north-east Ireland. *Ir. Nat. J.*, **15**: 267-269. ● Analyses of stomach contents and faeces.

263 **Fairley, J. S., 1967.**
Notes on the food of the fieldmouse in Irish woodland. *Ir. Nat. J.*, **15**: 300-302. ● Analyses of stomach contents.

264 **Fairley, J. S., 1967.**
The fieldmouse *Apodemus sylvaticus* (L.) in the Burren. *Ir. Nat. J.*, **15**: 330-331.

265 **Fairley, J. S., 1967.**
Wood mice in grassland at Dundrum, Co. Down, Northern Ireland. *J. Zool., Lond.*, **153**: 553-555. ● A population study.

266 **Fairley, J. S., 1967.**
A woodland population of *Apodemus sylvaticus* (L.) at Seaforde, Co. Down. *Proc. R. Ir. Acad.*, **65**B: 407-424.

267 **Fairley, J. S.,** 1969.
Destruction of foxes in Northern Ireland. *Ir. Nat. J.,* **16**: 187-189. ● Methods used and their effectiveness.

268 **Fairley, J. S.,** 1969.
Some field observations on the fox in Northern Ireland. *Ir. Nat. J.,* **16**: 189-192.

269 **Fairley, J. S.,** 1969.
Bank voles *Clethrionomys glareolus* Schr. in Co. Cork. *Ir. Nat. J.,* **16**: 209.

270 **Fairley, J. S.,** 1969.
A critical examination of the Northern Ireland fox bounty figures. *Ir. Nat. J.,* **16**: 213-215.

271 **Fairley, J. S.,** 1969.
The fox as a pest of agriculture. *Ir. Nat. J.,* **16**: 216-219.

272 **Fairley, J. S.,** 1969.
An exceptionally large fox. *Ir. Nat. J.,* **16**: 242-243.

273 **Fairley, J. S.,** 1969.
Injuries sustained by foxes. *Ir. Nat. J.,* **16**: 243.

274 **Fairley, J. S.,** 1969.
Tagging studies of the red fox *Vulpes vulpes* in northeast Ireland. *J. Zool., Lond.,* **159**: 527-532. ● Forty-seven discrete movements recorded by ear-tagging foxes.

275 **Fairley, J. S.,** 1969.
Survival of fox (*Vulpes vulpes*) cubs in Northern Ireland. *J. Zool., Lond.,* **159**: 532-534.

276 **Fairley, J. S., 1970.**
Some new records of fleas from Irish mammals. *Entomologist's Gaz.*, **21**: 21-22. ● Majority of records from foxes.

277 **Fairley, J. S., 1970.**
More records of fleas from Irish mammals. *Entomologist's Gaz.*, **21**: 295-299.

278 **Fairley, J. S., 1970.**
Blackberries as food of pine marten. *Ir. Nat. J.*, **16**: 317-318.

279 **Fairley, J. S., 1970.**
Epifauna from Irish bank voles. *Clethrionomys glareolus* Schreber. *Ir. Nat. J.*, **16**: 342-346.

280 **Fairley, J. S., 1970.**
New records of deer in Ireland. *Ir. Nat. J.*, **16**: 380.

281 **Fairley, J. S., 1970.**
Form of the fieldmouse *Apodemus sylvaticus* in Ireland. *Ir. Nat. J.*, **16**: 381. ● A brief summary of dimensions and coat colour of over 150 mice.

282 **Fairley, J. S., 1970.**
More results from tagging studies of foxes. *Vulpes vulpes* (L.). *Ir. Nat. J.*, **16**: 392-393.

283 **Fairley, J. S., 1970.**
Foetal number and resorption in wood mice from Ireland. *J. Zool., Lond.*, **161**: 276-277.

284 **Fairley, J. S., 1970.**
The food, reproduction, form, growth and develop-

ment of the fox *Vulpes vulpes* (L.) in north-east Ireland. *Proc. R. Ir. Acad.*, **69**B: 103-137. ● Extensive data from dissections of 800 foxes.

285 **Fairley, J. S.,** 1971.

More records of fleas from Irish mammals (second series). *Entomologist's Gaz.*, **22**: 259-263. ● Many from fieldmice.

286 **Fairley, J. S.,** 1971.

Malareus pencilliger mustelae (Dale), a flea new to Ireland. *Entomologist's mon., Mag.*, **107**: 44. ● From bank voles.

287 **Fairley, J. S.,** 1971.

A critical reappraisal of the status in Ireland of the eastern house mouse *Mus musculus orientalis* Cretzmar. *Ir. Nat. J.*, **17**: 2-5. ● The evidence for the races described in Nos. 664 and 666 is examined and these races shown to be artefacts.

288 **Fairley, J. S.,** 1971.

Bank vales *Clethrionomys glareolus* Schreber in Cos. Clare and Tipperary. *Ir. Nat. J.*, **17**: 23-24.

289 **Fairley, J. S.,** 1971.

New data on the Irish stoat. *Ir. Nat. J.*, **17**: 49-57. ● Fresh information on form, food, reproduction and parasites.

290 **Fairley, J. S.,** 1971.

Notes on the breeding of the fox (*Vulpes vulpes*) in Co. Galway, Ireland. *J. Zool., Lond.*, **164**: 262-263.

291 **Fairley, J. S.,** 1971.

The present distribution of the bank vole *Cleth-*

rionomys glareolus Schreber in Ireland. *Proc. R. Ir. Acad.*, **71**B: 183-189. ● Detailed distribution from trapping.

292 **Fairley, J. S., 1971.**
A collection of Irish bank vole skulls. *Scient. Proc. R. Dubl. Soc.*, **4**A: 37-44. ● Measurements reveal distinct differences from material measured elsewhere.

293 **Fairley, J. S., 1971.**
The control of fox *Vulpes vulpes* (L.) populations in Northern Ireland. *Scient. Proc. R. Dubl. Soc.*, **3**B: 43-47. ● Reviews possible limiting factors.

294 *****Fairley, J. S., 1972.**
The fieldmouse in Ireland. *Ir. Nat. J.*, **17**: 152-159. ● Review of the literature.

295 **Fairley, J. S., and Clark, F. L., 1971.**
Barn owl pellets from Co. Galway. *Br. Birds,* **64**: 34.

296 **Fairley, J. S. and Clark, F. L., 1971.**
A pilot whale *Globiocephala melaena* (Traill) stranded at Leagaun, Claddaghduff, Co. Galway. *Ir. Nat. J.*, **17**: 103.

297 **Fairley, J. S. and Comerton, M. E., 1972.**
An early-breeding population of fieldmice *Apodemus sylvaticus* (L.) in Limekiln Wood, Athenry, Co. Galway. *Proc. R. Ir. Acad.*, **72**B: 149-163.

298 **Fairley, J. S. and Deane, C. D., 1967.**
Analysis of barn owl pellets from Co. Fermanagh. *Br. Birds,* **60**: 370.

299   **Fairley, J. S. and McLean, A.,** 1965.
Notes on the summer food of the kestrel in northern Ireland. *Br. Birds*, **58**: 145-148. ● Analyses of pellets.

300   **Fairley, J. S., and O'Donnell, T.,** 1970.
The distribution of the bank vole *Clethrionomys glareolus* in south-west Ireland. *J. Zool., Lond.*, **161**: 273-276. ● From trapping.

301   **Fairley, J. S. and O'Gorman, F. L.,** 1971.
Barn owl, *Tyto alba* (Scopoli), pellets from Co. Wicklow. *Ir. Nat. J.*, **17**: 62.

302   **Faris, R. C.,** 1948.
Bats drinking. *Ir. Nat. J.*, **9**: 123-124.

303   **Farran, G. P.,** 1904.
A black rat on board ship. *Ir. Nat.*, **13**: 48.

304   **Farran, G. P.,** 1915.
Results of a biological survey of Blacksod Bay, Co. Mayo. *Scient. Invest. Fish. Brch Ire.*, **3**: 1-72. ● Includes a note on whale-fisheries.

305   **Farrington, A.,** 1946.
Flight of bats. *Ir. Nat. J.*, **8**: 394-395.

306   **Fermoy, Lord.,** 1888.
Speed and weight of the Irish hare. *Field*, **71**: 527. ● Imported brown, and white Irish hares.

307   **Fetherston, H. G.,** 1885.
Accident to a hare. *Field*, **66**: 349. ● Hare injures itself.

308 **F. H.,** 1874.
The Irish hare. *Field,* **44**: 116.

309 **Fisher, N.,** 1934.
The last Irish wolf. *Ir. Nat. J.,* **5**: 41.

310 **Fitter, R. S. R.,** 1964.
Irish otters and deer in danger. *Wld Wildl. News,* **22**: 5.

311 **Flemyng, W. W.,** 1894.
Habits of the badger. *Zoologist,* (3) **18**: 186.

312 **Flemyng, W. W.,** 1895.
Occurrence of the marten in Co. Waterford. *Ir. Nat.,* **4**: 224.

313 **Flemyng, W. W.,** 1895.
Marten in Co. Waterford. *Zoologist,* (3) **19**: 301-302.

314 **Flemyng, W. W.,** 1897.
Marten in the County Waterford. *Zoologist,* (4) **1**: 141.

315 **Flemyng, W. W.,** 1897.
Pine marten in the County Waterford. *Zoolog:st,* (4) **1**: 327.

316 **Flemyng, W. W.,** 1899.
Long-eared bat in Co. Waterford. *Ir. Nat.,* **8**: 61.

317 **Flemyng, W. W.,** 1913.
A gamekeeper's list of undesirables. *Ir. Nat.,* **22**: 162-163. ● Kills on an Irish estate over one year.

Fletcher, G. (ed.) 1921-22. See No. 751.

318 **Flynn, J. E., 1935.**
The lesser horse-shoe bat (*Rhinolophus hipposideros*) in Co. Cork. *Ir. Nat. J.*, **5**: 228-229.

319 **Foot, F. J., 1859, 1860.**
Description of Balliallia Cave, Ennis, with account of the discovery of the lesser horse-shoe bat. *Proc. Dubl. nat. Hist. Soc.*, (1860) **2**: 152-154. Also in *Nat. Hist. Rev.*, (Proceedings of the Societies section) (1859) **6**: 379-381.

320 **Foot, F. J., 1863.**
Natural history notes on the Mammalia of the west coast of Clare. *Proc. Dubl. nat. Hist. Soc.*, **3**: 104-106.

321 **Forbes, A. C., 1937.**
The pine marten in Co. Wexford. *Ir. Nat. J.*, **6**: 301.

322 **Forbes, A. C., 1943.**
Some early economic and other developments in Eire and their effect on forestry conditions. *Ir. For.*, **1**: 6-15. ● Rabbits, deer.

323 **Forbes, A. R., 1905.**
Gaelic Names of Beasts (Mammalia), Birds, Fishes, Insects, Reptiles etc. Oliver and Boyd. Edinburgh. ● Nomenclature only.

324 ***Forrest, H. E., 1908.**
Vertebrates of Wales and Ireland. *Zoologist*, (4) **12**: 321-325, 454. ● A comparison.

325 **Forrest, H. E., 1926.**
Prehistoric mammals of Ireland. *Ir. Nat. J.*, **1**: 112-

114, 152-153, 171-174, 215-219, 228, 234-236, 259-262, 284-285. ● Review.

326 **Forrest, H. E., 1928.**
The hare in the Isle of Man. *Ir. Nat. J.*, **2**: 44. ● Correspondence on the mammal fauna of Ireland compared with that on the Isle of Man. See also No. 609.

327 **Foster, N. H., 1904.**
Bat abroad in bright sunlight. *Ir. Nat. J.*, **13**: 120.

328 **Foster, N. H., 1917.**
The Mourne Mountains. *Proc. Belf. Nat. Fld Club*, (2) **7**: 294-296. ● Brief reference to foxes and badgers indicating their scarcity in northern Ireland at the time.

329 **Foster, N. H., 1922.**
Hairy-armed bat in Co. Down. *Ir. Nat. J.*, **31**: 35.

330 **Foster, N. H., 1923.**
The fox in Co. Down. *Ir. Nat.*, **32**: 96.

331 **Foyle Fisheries Commission, 1958-70.**
Foyle Fish. Comm. Rep., 7-19. ● These list numbers of bounties paid on otters (to 1968) and seals (to date), occasionally with remarks.

332 **Fraser, F. C., 1934-53.**
Rep. Cetacea Br. Csts, **11-13**. ● Much valuable data for years 1927-47. Continued from No. 394.

333 **Fraser, F. C., 1940.**
Three anomalous dolphins from Blacksod Bay, Ireland. *Proc. R. Ir. Acad.*, **45**B: 413-455.

334 **Fraser, F. C., 1942.**

The mesorostral ossification of *Ziphius cavirostris*. *Proc. zool. Soc. Lond.*, **112**B: 21-30. ● Some detail on an Irish specimen.

335 **Fraser, F. C., 1945.**

Cetacea stranded on the British coast during 1944. *Ann. Mag. nat. Hist.*, (11) **12**: 347-350.

336 **Fraser, F. C., 1957.**

Cetaceans stranded on the British coasts during 1956. *Bull. Mammal Soc. Br. Isles*, **7**: 21-22.

337 **Fraser, F. C., 1959.**

Cetaceans stranded on the British coasts during 1957 and 1958. *Bull. Mammal Soc. Br. Isles*, **11**: 15-17.

338 **Fraser, F. C., 1960.**

Cetaceans stranded on the British coasts during 1959. *Bull. Mammal Soc. Br. Isles*, **13**: 22-23.

339 **Fraser, F. C., 1963.**

List of whales stranded on British coasts during 1962. *Bull. Mammal Soc. Br. Isles*, **10**: 12.

340 **Freeman, R. B., 1940.**

Orchopeas wickhami (Baker) (Siphonaptera) in Ireland. *Entomologist's mon. Mag.*, **76**: 205-206. ● From grey squirrel.

341 **Freeman, R. B., 1941.**

The distribution of *Orchopeas wickhami* (Baker) (Siphonaptera), in relation to its host the American grey squirrel. *Entomologist's mon. Mag.*, **72**: 82-89.

342 **Freeman, R. B.,** 1946.
Nyteridopsylla longiceps Roths. (Siph. Ischnopsyl·
lidae) in Ireland. *Entomologist's mon. Mag.,* **82**: 117
● Bat flea.

343 **F. S. H.,** 1881.
Curious capture of a seal. *Field,* **58**: 962. ● Seal takes
fishing bait.

344 **Furnell, M. J. G.,** 1957.
The incidence of trichinosis in Ireland. *Rep. med.
Res. Coun. Ire.,* (1957): 43-44. ● Rats infected with
Trichinella.

345 **F. W. B.,** 1902.
A hybrid deer at Powerscourt. *Field,* **100**: 1012.

346 **'Gamekeeper',** 1874.
Marten cats in Ireland. *Field,* **43**: 347.

347 **Garnett, H.,** 1929.
Wild nature on the Saltee Islands. *Ir. Nat. J.,* **2**: 235-
236. ● Some mammals listed.

348 **Garvey, T.,** 1935.
The musk rat in Saorstat Éireann. *J. Dep. Agric. Re-
pub. Ire.,* **33**: 189-195.

349 **Gatcombe, J.,** 1875.
Hairy-armed bat in the County Armagh. *Zoologist,*
(2) **10**: 4419.

350 **Gethin, R. G.,** 1936.
Pine marten visitor. *Ir. Nat. J.,* **6**: 145-146.

351   **Gibbon, E. A., 1901.**
Bat catching flies in day-time. *Ir. Nat.,* **10**: 175.

352   **'Gillaro', 1870.**
Large otter. *Field,* **35**: 273.

353   **Gilmore, R. M., 1899.**
Pine marten and common badger in County Galway.
Ir. Nat., **8**: 252.

354   **Gilmore, R. M., 1900.**
The hooded seal reported from Galway Bay. *Ir. Nat.,*
9: 82.

355   **Giraldus Cambrensis, c. 1185.**
Topographica Hibernica. (Several translations e.g.
Wright, T., 1892. *The Historical Works of Giraldus
Cambrensis.* Bell. London.). ● Some Irish mammals
discussed. Much of the account is apocryphal.

356   **Glendinning, J., and Glendinning, E., 1926.**
Hedgehogs. *Ir. Nat. J.,* **1**: 91. ● Anecdotal. Little zoological interest.

357   **Government of Northern Ireland, 1953-65.**
Ulster Yr Bk, (1953, 1957-59, 1960-62, 1963-65). ●
These list numbers of bounties paid on foxes in N.
Ireland.

358   **Gray, J. E., 1846.**
On the British Cetacea. *Ann. Mag. nat. Hist.,* **17**: 82-
85.

359   ***Gray, J. E., 1866.**
Catalogue of Seals and Whales in the British Mus-

eum. (Second edition). British Museum (Natural History). London.

360 **Gray, J. E., 1872.**
Ziphius sowerbiensis. Ann. Mag. nat. Hist., (4) **10**: 151. ● Records specimen in National Museum, Dublin. No provenance.

361 **Gray, J. E., 1873.**
Catalogue of the whales and dolphins (Cetacea) inhabiting or incidentally visiting the seas surrounding the British Isles. *Zoologist,* (2) **8**: 3357-3364, 3421-3433. ● Little on Irish whales.

362 **Granard, Lord, 1936.**
Pine marten in Co. Longford. *Field,* **67**: 955.

363 **Greer, T., 1923.**
Foxes in Co. Tyrone. *Ir. Nat.,* **32**: 116.

364 ***Gresson, R. A. R., 1954.**
The food of badgers. *Ir. Nat. J.,* **11**: 203-205. ● Brief review of British work and comment on its application to Ireland.

365 **Gresson, R. A. R., 1966.**
Pilot whales, *Globiocephala melaena* (Triall), stranded at Cloghane, Co. Kerry. *Ir. Nat. J.,* **15**: 163-166. ● Sixty-three whales stranded.

366 **Gresson, R. A. R., 1968.**
White-sided dolphins, *Lagenorhynchus acutus* (Gray) stranded at Ventry Harbour, Co. Kerry. *Ir. Nat. J.,* **16**: 19-20.

367 **Gresson, R. A. R.,** 1969.
White-sided dolphins *Lagenorhynchus acutus* (Gray) stranded at Brandon Bay, Co. Kerry. *Ir. Nat. J.,* **16:** 140.

368 **Gresson, R. A. R.,** 1969.
A pilot whale, *Globiocephala melaena* (Triall) on Fermoyle Strand, Co. Kerry. *Ir. Nat. J.,* **16:** 141.

369 **Gresson, R. A. R.,** 1969.
White-sided dolphins, *Lagenorhynchus actus* (Gray) stranded at Cloghane, Co. Kerry, *Ir. Nat. J.,* **16:** 228.

370 **Gresson, R. A. R. and O'Riordan, C. E.,** 1969.
Carcase of True's beaked whale, *Mesoplodon mirus* True, near Dingle, Co. Kerry. *Ir. Nat. J.,* **16:** 226-227.

371 **Griffith, H. A. C.,** 1927.
Otters in County Down. *Ir. Nat. J.,* **1:** 275.

372 **Grub, J.,** 1862.
The wolf-days of Ireland. *Zoologist,* **20:** 7996-7997.

373 **Gulliver, G.,** 1853.
Notes on a cetaceous animal stranded on the north-east coast of Ireland. *Proc. zool. Soc. Lond.,* (1853): 63-67.

374 **Gumley, E. M.,** 1929.
The common rat. *Ir. Nat. J.,* **2:** 171-172. ● Correspondence on '*Mus hibernicus*' specimens.

375 **Gunning, B. E. S. and Pate, J. S.,** 1954.
Golden eagle in County Antrim. *Ir. Nat. J.,* **11:** 208.

● Eagle eats rabbit. Detailed description of uneaten portions.

Guy and Co. See No. 580.

376 **Gyles, G.,** 1883.
Homing instinct in bats. *Zoologist,* (3) **7**: 173.

377 **Hackett, W. A.,** 1873.
Otter in a lobster pot. *Field,* **42**: 138.

378 **Hackett, W. A.,** 1875.
Large whales off Cork Harbour. *Field,* **46**: 75. ● Account of collision between whale and ship.

379 **Hackett, W. A.,** 1875.
Whales. *Field,* **46**: 183. ● Unidentified whales sighted.

380 **Hackett, W. A.,** 1875.
Marten cats in Co. Cork. *Field,* **46**: 390.

381 **Hackett, W. A.,** 1865.
Bittern and marten cat in Co. Cork. *Field,* **46**: 416.

382 **Hackett, W. A.,** 1879.
Marten cat in Co. Cork. *Field,* **53**: 625.

383 **Haigh, G. H. C.,** 1895.
Irish hare turning white in winter. *Zoologist,* (3) **19**: 185-186.

384 **Halbert, J. N.,** 1915.
Acarinida 2. Terrestrial and marine. Clare Island Survey. Part 39. Section ii. *Proc. R. Ir. Acad.,* **31**: 45-136. ● Mites and ticks from rodents and bats.

385 **Halbert, J. N., 1923.**
Notes on Acari with descriptions of new species. *J. Linn. Soc. (Zool.).* **35**: 363-392. ● Includes mites from fieldmouse.

Halbert, J. N., 1935. See No. 125.

386 **Haldane, R. C., 1909.**
Whaling in Scotland for 1908. *Ann. Scot. nat. Hist.,* **18**: 65-69. ● Catch at an Irish fishery included.

387 **Hall, Z., 1956.**
Leisler's bat in Co. Dublin. *Ir. Nat. J.,* **12**: 42.

388 **Hamilton, E., 1885.**
Remarks on the supposed existence of the wild cat (*Felis cattus*) in Ireland. *Proc. zool. Soc. Lond.,* (1885): 211-214.

389 **Hamilton, E., 1896.**
The Wild Cat of Europe. Porter. London.

390 **Hamilton, J. E., 1915.**
Belmullet whaling station. Report to the committee. *Rep. Br. Ass. Advmt Sci.,* (Australia: 1914): 125-161. ● A comprehensive report covering many aspects of whales and whale-fishing.

391 **Hamilton, J. E., 1916.**
Belmullet whaling station. Report of the committee. *Rep. Br. Ass. Advmt Sci.,* (Manchester: 1915): 124-146. ● As last reference.

392 **Hamilton, Marquis of., 1902.**
Weight of fallow deer. *Field,* **100**: 681.

393 **Hamilton, Marquis of,** 1905.
Pine marten in Co. Tyrone. *Field,* **105**: 73.

394 **Harmer, S. F.,** 1914-27.
Rep. Cetacea Br. Csts, **1-10**. ● Much valuable data
for the years 1913-26. Continued in No. 332.

395 **Harmer, S. F.,** 1915.
On the specimens of Cuvier's whale (*Ziphius cavir-
orostris*) from the Irish coast. *Proc. zool. Soc. Lond.,*
(1915): 559-566.

396 ***Harris, C. J.,** 1968.
Otters. Weidenfeld and Nicolson. London. ● Nothing
original but reviews much of the Irish information
in detail.

397 **Hart, H. C.,** 1891.
Natterer's bat in Co. Donegal. *Zoologist,* (3) **15**: 271.

398 **Hart, H. C.,** 1894.
The marten in Co. Donegal. *Ir. Nat.,* **3**: 158.

399 **Hart, H. C.,** 1899.
Lesser rorqual in the Swilly. *Ir. Nat.,* **8**: 28. ● Dis-
puted in No. 78.

400 **Hart, W. E.,** 1901.
Winter flight of bats. *Ir. Nat.,* **10**: 51.

401 **Harting, J. E.,** 1873.
Marten cats robbing hives. *Field,* **41**: 478. ● Heresay.

402 **Harting, J. E.,** 1880.
British Animals Extinct within Historic Times. Trüb-
ner. London. ● Wolves.

403 **Harting, J. E., 1883.**
Essays on Sport and Natural History. Cox. London.
● General. Includes an excellent review of the earliest works on Irish natural history.

404 **Harting, J. E., 1886.**
Irish deer. *Field,* **68**: 884. ● Records wild fallow deer in the west.

405 **Harting, J. E., 1889.**
Mus hibernicus, Thompson, restored to the British fauna. *Zoologist,* (3) **13**: 199-206.

406 **Harting J. E., 1889.**
Natterer's bat, *Vespertilio nattereri. Zoologist,* (3) **13**: 241-248. ● Includes distribution in Ireland.

407 **Harting, J. E., 1891.**
The marten in Co. Down. *Zoologist,* (3) **15**: 304.

408 ***Harting, J. E., 1894.**
The otter *Lutra vulgaris. Zoologist* (3) **18**: 1-10, 41-47, 379-385. ● Reviews some Irish references.

409 **Harting, J. E., 1894.**
The marten in Ireland. *Zoologist,* (3) **18**: 100-107. ● Numerous records.

410 **Harting, J. E., 1894.**
Destruction of martens in Ireland. *Zoologist,* (3) **18**: 222-223.

411 **Harting, J. E., 1894.**
The weasel. *Zoologist,* (3) **18**: 417-423, 445-454. ● Notes on possible Irish records.

412 **Harting, J. E., 1895.**
The harvest mouse. *Zoologist* (3) **19**: 418-425. ● Not present in Ireland.

413 **Harting, J. E., 1903.**
Japanese and red deer hybrid. *Field,* **102**: 763.

414 **Harvey, J. R., 1845.**
Contributions towards a Fauna and Flora of the County of Cork: Vertebrata. Van Voorst. London. Purcell. Cork. ● Read at the British Association meeting in Cork. N.B. This is only noticed in *Rep. Br. Ass. Advmt Sci.* (Cork: 1843).

415 **Harvey, J. R. (in Cusack, M. F.), 1875.**
A History of the City and County of Cork. McGlashen and Gill. Dublin. Guy. Cork. ● Includes a list of mammals similar to that in the last reference.

416 **Harvie-Brown, J. A., 1881.**
The History of the Squirrel in Great Britain. M'Farlane and Erskine. Edinburgh. ● Includes several remarks on Irish squirrels.

417 **Harvie-Brown, J. A., 1913.**
Wild cats in Ireland. *Ir. Nat.,* **22**: 125-126.

Harvie-Brown, J. A. and Buckley, T. E., 1892. See No. 747.

418 **Hearns, P., 1862.**
An otter-fight with two salmon. *Field,* **20**: 459.

419 **Hedges, S. R., 1969.**
Epigenetic polymorphism in populations of *Apode-*

mus sylvaticus and *Apodemus flavicollis* (Rodentia, Muridae). *J. Zool., Lond.,* **159**: 425-442.

420 **Henderson, J. A.,** 1947.
Grey squirrel in Co. Fermanagh. *Ir. Nat. J.,* **9**: 97. ● Records.

421 **Herbert, T.,** 1885.
Wolves in Ireland. *Zoologist,* (3) **9**: 268.

422 **Heron, E. D.,** 1929-30.
Unusually coloured wild mice. *Ir. Nat. J.,* **2**: 212; **3**: 48. ● Semi-albino house mice.

423 **Heron, G. E.,** 1962.
Beechmast hoard. *Countryman, Idbury,* **59**: 103. ● Belonged to fieldmouse.

424 **Hewer, H. R.,** 1955.
Marking of Atlantic seals. *Bull. Mammal Soc. Br. Isles,* **4**: 20-22. ● Same results as in next reference.

425 **Hewer, H. R.,** 1955.
Notes on the marking of Atlantic seals in Pembrokeshire. *Proc. zool. Soc. Lond.,* **125**: 87-93. ● Recovery from Ireland.

426 *****Hewer, H. R.,** 1962.
Grey seals. Sunday Times Publications. London. (Animals of Britain No. 7).

427 **Hillis, J. P.,** 1966.
White-sided dolphin, *Lagenorhynchus acutus* from Co. Donegal. *Ir. Nat. J.,* **15**: 212.

428 Hinton, M. A. C., 1909.
On the fossil hare of the ossiferous fissures of Ignatham, Kent, and on the recent hares of the *Lepus variabilis* group. *Scient. Proc. R. Dubl. Soc.*, (n.s.) **12**: 225-265.

429 Hinton, M. A. C., 1914.
Notes on the British forms of Apodemus. *Ann. Mag. nat. Hist.*, (9) **14**: 117-134. ● Includes a few measurements of a skull from Inishmore Island.

430 Hinton, M. A. C., 1920.
The Irish otter. *Ann. Mag. nat. Hist.*, (9) **5**: 464.

431 Hope, E., 1906.
Fawn coloured Irish hares. *Field*, **107**: 442.

432 Hopkins, G. H. E. and Rothschild, M., 1953-71.
An Illustrated Catalogue of the Rothschild Collection of Fleas (Siphonaptera) in the British Museum (Natural History). *London*. Vols. 1-5. University Press. Cambridge.

433 Hore, P. H., 1917.
Ferae Naturae in County Wexford. *Selbourne Mag.*, **28**: 9. ● Local mammal fauna.

434 H. R. P., 1878.
Otters in Kerry. *Field*, **51**: 245. ● Weight of large specimen.

435 Humphreys, G. R., 1910.
Marten in Co. Galway. *Ir. Nat.*, **19**: 140.

436 **Hunter, S. A.,** 1934.
Parasites of a badger. *Ir. Nat. J.,* **5**: 72. ● Lice and a flea.

437 **Hurley, S. J.,** 1885.
Tame otters. *Field,* **66**: 776. ● Anecdotal.

438 **Hurley, S. J.,** 1887.
Otters in the Shannon. *Field,* **69**: 54, 110.

439 **Hurley, S. J.,** 1892.
The otter. *Ir. Sportsman,* **23**: 380. ● Correspondence on breeding.

440 **Hurley, S. J.,** 1898.
White otters. *Field,* **91**: 142.

441 **Hutchinson, A. S.,** 1889.
Martens in County Kerry. *Field,* **73**: 801.

442 **Hutchinson, W. F.,** 1880.
A foundling otter. *Field,* **56**: 320.

443 **'Inquirer',** 1874.
Supposed hybrid between dog and fox. *Field,* **43**: 444. ● See No. 466.

444 **Irwin, R. B.,** 1896.
Weasel in a woodpigeon's nest. *Field,* **88**: 221. ● Stoat, not a weasel.

445 **J. A. B.,** 1893.
A marten (*Mustela martes*) in Co. Antrim. *Ir. Nat.,* **2**: 202.

446 **J. A. B., 1894.**
The badger in Co. Tyrone. *Land Wat.,* **57**: 57.

447 **Jackson, J. S., 1961.**
Two records of grey squirrel, *Sciurus carolinensis* Gmelin, shot in counties Armagh and Monaghan. *Ir. Nat. J.,* **13**: 215.

448 **Jackson, J. S., 1961.**
Record of a long-eared bat, *Plecotus auritus* (Linnaeus) from County Clare. *Ir. Nat. J.,* **13**: 262-263.

449 **Jacob, A., 1825.**
On the generic characters and anatomical structure of the whale, entitled *Delphinus diodon* by Hunter, and *Hyperoodon* by La Cepede. *Dubl. Phil. J.,* **1**: 58-73. ● Stranding.

450 **Jacob, A., 1825.**
Account of a whale which was found floating in the Atlantic Ocean on the north-west coast of Ireland; with some observations respecting its generic characters and anatomical structure. *Dubl. Phil. J.,* **1**: 333-350.

451 **Jameson, H. L., 1893.**
The reddish-grey bat (*Vespertilio nattereri*) in Co. Louth. *Ir. Nat.,* **2**: 230.

452 **Jameson, H. L., 1894.**
Irish bats. *Ir. Nat.,* **3**: 69-71.

453 **Jameson, H. L., 1897.**
The bats of Ireland. *Ir. Nat.,* **6**: 34-43. ● Known records listed and many new ones added.

454   **Jameson, H. L., 1897.**
      Irish bats. *Ir. Nat.*, **6**: 135.

455   **Jameson, H. L., 1898.**
      On a probable case of protective coloration in the
      house-mouse (*Mus musculus* Linn.) *J. Linn. Soc.*, **26**:
      456-473. ● On Bull Island.

456   **J. B. D., 1896.**
      The weasel in Ireland. *Field*, **88**: 607. ● Supposed re-
      cords.

457   **J. C., 1922.**
      Hares in the city of Belfast. *Ir. Nat.*, **31**: 84.

458   **Jenkins, J. T., 1921.**
      A History of Whale Fisheries. Witherby. London. ●
      Lists numbers of whales caught at Irish fisheries
      1909-1920.

459   **Jenner, B. St. A., 1908.**
      Long-eared bat in Kerry. *Field*, **112**: 291.

460   **Jenner, B. St. A., 1908.**
      The squirrel in Co. Kerry. *Field*, **112**: 721.

461   **Jenyns, L. J., 1835.**
      A Manual of British Vertebrate Animals. Pitt Press.
      Cambridge. ● A very few references to Ireland.

462   **Jenyns, L. J., 1838.**
      Further remarks on the British shrews, including
      the distinguishing characters of two species pre-
      viously confounded. *Ann. Mag. nat. Hist.*, **1**: 418-427.
      ● An alleged new Irish variety of the pigmy shrew.

463 **Jenyns, L. J., 1841.**
Notes on some of the smaller British Mammalia, including the description of a new species of *Arvicola* found in Scotland. *Ann. Mag. nat. Hist.*, **7**: 261-267.
● Bats. Fieldmice at high altitude.

464 **Jewell, P. A. and Fullagar, P. J., 1965.**
Fertility among races of field mouse (*Apodemus sylvaticus*) and their failure to form hybrids with the yellow-necked mouse (*Apodemus flavicollis*). *Evolution, Lancaster, Pa.*, **19**: 175-181.

465 **J. G., 1900.**
Young badgers. *Field,* **95**: 579.

466 **J. H. J., 1874.**
Supposed hybrid between dog and fox. *Field,* **43**: 431.
● See No. 443.

467 **Johnson, W. F., 1904.**
A bat on the wing in December. *Ir. Nat. J.*, **13**: 49.

468 **Johnson, W. F., 1915.**
Robin and mouse. *Ir. Nat.*, **24**: 217.

469 ***Johnson, Sir H., 1903.**
British Mammals. Hutchinson. London.

470 **J. R. T. M., 1901.**
Hare chased by otter. *Field,* **97**: 442.

471 **Kane, W. F. de V., 1894.**
The reddish-grey bat (*Vespertilio nattereri*, Kuhl) in Co. Galway. *Ir. Nat.*, **3**: 116.

472 **Kane, W. F. de V.,** 1896.

Pine martens recently taken in Ireland. *Ir. Nat.,* **5**: 28.

473 **Kane, W. F. de V.,** 1897.

Irish bats. *Ir. Nat.,* **6**: 88. ● Includes record from Blasket Islands.

474 **Kane, W. F. de V.,** 1905.

Wild cats formerly indigenous in Ireland. *Ir. Nat.,* **14**: 165-166.

475 **Kane, W. F. de V.,** 1915.

The natural history of Antrim. *Selbourne Mag.,* **26**: 124. ● Quotes from early manuscript of W. Molyneux on the natural history of Leitrim *not* Antrim. Deer, wolves.

476 **'Keeper',** 1895.

Weight of badger. *Field,* **85**: 152. ● Large badger.

477 **'Keeper',** 1897.

Marten in County Waterford. *Field,* **90**: 1018.

478 **Kelsall, J. E.,** 1887.

The distribution in Great Britain of the lesser horseshoe bat. *Zoologist,* (3) **11**: 89-93. ● Includes Ireland. New record from Co. Kerry and nycteribiid parasite.

479 **Keogh, J.,** 1739.

Zoologia Medicinalis Hibernica. Powell. Dublin.

480 **Ker, E.,** 1874.

Irish hare turning white in winter—badgers and otters in Ireland. *Field,* **44**: 81.

481 **Kinahan, J. R., 1853.**

Occurrence of the reddish gray bat (*Vespertilio nattereri*) in Ireland. *Zoologist,* **11**: 4012-4013.

482 **Kinahan, J. R., 1854.**

(Exhibition and notes on an unidentified bat). *Proc. Dubl. Univ. zool. Ass. in Nat. Hist. Rev.,* (Proceedings of the Societies section) **1**: 87.

483 **Kinahan, J. R., 1854, 1858.**

On the occurrence of Natterer's bat in the County Kildare. *Proc. Dubl. nat. Hist. Soc.,* (1858) **1**: 66-69. Also in *Nat. Hist. Rev.,* (Proceedings of the Societies section) (1854) **1**: 23-25. ● Includes notes on other local mammals.

484 **Kinahan, J. R., 1859, 1860.**

Mammalogica Hibernica: Part 1.—Sub-Class, Lissencephala; Order Cheiroptera, Insectivoridae;—or, a general review of the history and distribution of bats in Ireland; with remarks on Mr. Foot's discovery in Clare of the lesser horse-shoe bat, a species hitherto unrecorded in Ireland. *Proc. Dubl. nat. Hist. Soc.,* (1860) **2**: 154-170. Also in *Nat. Hist. Rev.,* (Proceedings of the Societies section) (1859) **6**: 381-397. ● A comprehensive account.

485 **Kinahan, J. R., 1860, 1863.**

Addendum to Mammalogica Hibernica—Cheiroptera. *Proc. Dubl. nat. Hist. Soc.,* (1863) **3**: 42-43. Also in *Nat. Hist. Rev.,* (Proceedings of the Societies section) (1860) **7**: 396-397.

486 **Kinahan, J. R., 1861, 1863.**

Three days amongst the bats of Clare. *Proc. Dubl.*

nat. Hist. Soc., (1863) **3**: 94-99. Also in *Dubl. Q. Jl Sci.*, (1863) **3**: 1-7 and *Zoologist,* (1861) **19**: 7617-7624.

487 **Kinahan, G. H., 1892.**
Piebald stoats—Migration of curlew. *Land. Wat.*, **53**: 643.

488 **Kinahan, G. H., 1892.**
White and pied stoats. *Zoologist,* (3) **16**: 265. ● Very similar to part of previous reference.

489 **Kinahan, G. H., 1896.**
On possible land connections, in recent geological times, between Ireland and Great Britain. *Manchr. geol. Min. Soc. Trans.*, **24**: 113-128. ● On the time of origin of the Irish fauna, especially mammals.

490 **King, A. L. K., 1952.**
Pine marten in Roscommon. *Ir. Nat. J.*, **10**: 321.

491 **King, W., 1859.**
On the occurence in Galway of the lesser horse-shoe bat (*Rhinolophis hipposideros*). *Proc. Dubl. Univ. zool. bot. Ass.*, **1**: 264-268. Also in *Nat. Hist. Rev.*, (Proceedings of the Societies section) **6**: 522-525.

492 **Knox, A., 1875.**
A History of the County of Down. Hodges and Foster. Dublin. ● Includes original notes on most of the local mammals.

493 **Knox, A. E., 1850.**
Game Birds and Wild Fowl: their Friends and their

Foes. Van Voorst. London. ● Very brief references to increase in hares and to wild cats.

494 **Knox, A. E.,** 1863.
Remarks on the date of the extinction of the mole and weasel in Ireland. *Proc. zool. Soc. Lond.,* (1863): 510. ● Title only.

495 **Knox, A. G.,** 1969.
A skull of Cuvier's whale found at Naran, W. Donegal. *Ir. Nat. J.,* **16**: 177.

496 **Lang, J. T.,** 1970.
Red deer, *Cervus elaphus,* in Wicklow. *Ir. Nat. J.,* **16**: 317. ● Sightings and numbers in herds.

497 **Langfield, R. E.,** 1901.
Stoat swallowed by a pike. *Field,* **98**: 312.

498 **Langam, C.,** 1896.
Whiskered bat in Co. Fermanagh. *Zoologist,* (3) **20**: 350.

499 **Langham, C.,** 1916.
Squirrel eating *Melanogaster ambiguus. Ir. Nat.,* **25**: 136.

500 **Langham, C.,** 1921.
Bats in Co. Fermanagh. *Ir. Nat.,* **30**: 26-27. ● New records of a few species.

501 **La Touche, M.,** 1886.
Habits of the squirrel. *Field,* **67**: 279.

502 **L. D.,** 1874.
Early broods of wild ducks and otters. *Field,* **43**: 445.

503 **L. D.,** 1874.
The Irish hare. *Field,* **44**: 171.

504 **Lees, G. I. D.,** 1894.
The last wolf killed in Ireland. *Land. Wat.,* **58**: 611, 689.

505 **Le Fanu, T. V.,** 1893.
The royal forest of Glencree. *J. R. Soc. Antiquaries Ire.,* (5) **3**: 268-280. ● Records an early import of deer.

506 **Le Fanu, T. V.,** 1922.
The squirrel in Ireland. *Ir. Nat.,* **31**: 83-84.

507 **'Lepus Hibernicus',** 1891.
Turning down Irish hares. *Field,* **78**: 174.

508 **'Lepus Hibernicus',** 1891.
The Irish hare *Lepus variabilis* Pallas. *Ir. Sportsman,* **22**: 428, 444, 486, 508. ● Considerable detail on various aspects.

509 ***'Lepus Hibernicus',** 1891.
Notes on Irish mammals—Sibbald's Rorqual. *Ir. Sportsman,* **22**: 620-621.

510 **'Lepus Hibernicus',** 1891.
The Alexandrine rat (*Mus alexandrinus*) in Ireland. *Ir. Sportsman,* **22**: 697.

511 **'Lepus Hibernicus',** 1891.
Lesser rorqual in Kerry. *Ir. Sportsman,* **22**: 697. ●
Stranding.

512 **'Lepus Hibernicus',** 1892.
White hares near Armagh. *Ir. Sportsman,* **22**: 829.

513 **'Lepus Hibernicus',** 1892.
Notes on the breeding of the otter. *Ir. Sportsman,* **23**: 327.

514 **'Lepus Hibernicus',** 1892.
The winter whitening of the stoat in Ireland. *Land. Wat.,* **53**: 590.

515 **'Lepus Hibernicus',** 1893.
Squirrel taking refuge in a rabbit burrow. *Land. Wat.,* **55**: 196.

516 **'Lepus Hibernicus',** 1894.
The last wolf killed in Ireland. *Land. Wat.,* **58**: 690.

517 **Leslie, J.,** 1931.
Liberation of greater horseshoe bats in Co. Monaghan, and other bat notes. *Ir. Nat. J.,* **3**: 222-223.

518 **Leslie, J.,** 1932.
Natterer's bat in Co. Monaghan and suggestion for barn owl census. *Ir. Nat. J.,* **4**: 124.

519 **Lett, H. W.,** 1895.
Irish rat (*Mus hibernicus* Thomps.) at Lough Brickland, Co. Down. *Ir. Nat.,* **4**: 80.

520 **Lett, W. H.,** 1901.
The occurrence of Natterer's bat and the whiskered bat in Co. Down. *Proc. Belf. Nat. Fld Club*, (2) **4**: 602-603.

521 **Lett, W. H.,** 1912.
Squirrels in Co. Louth. *Ir. Nat.,* **21**: 246.

522 **Levinge, H. C.,** 1895.
Marten in Co. Westmeath. *Ir. Nat.,* **4**: 21. A practically identical paper is published in *Zoologist,* (3) **18**: 423.

523 **Lillie, D. G.,** 1910.
Observations on the anatomy and general biology of some members of the larger Cetacea. *Proc. zool. Soc. Lond.,* (1910): 769-792. ● An important paper on many aspects of the whales caught at an Irish whaling station. (This work is noted in *Rep. Br. Ass. Advmt Sci.,* (Sheffield: 1910): 168-169 but no details are given).

524 **Lloyd, W. W.,** 1887.
Fearlessness of a seal. *Field,* **70**: 711.

525 **Lockley, R. M.,** 1954.
The Seals and the Curragh. Dent. London. ● Narrative.

526 **Lockley, R. M.,** 1954.
The Atlantic grey seal. *Oryx,* **2**: 384-387.

527 *****Lockley, R. M.,** 1966.
Grey Seal, Common Seal. Deutsch. London.

528 **Lockley, R. M.,** 1966.
The distribution of grey and common seals on the coasts of Ireland. *Ir. Nat. J.,* **15**: 136-143. ● The only comprehensive study.

529 **Lockley, R. M.,** 1966.
The seals of Wales and Ireland: their distribution and conservation. *Nature Wales,* **10**: 58-64.

530 **Loewenthal, J. E.,** 1922.
Hares in the city of Belfast. *Ir. Nat.,* **31**: 84.

531 **Lowenthal, J. E.,** 1924.
Squirrels near the central area of Belfast. *Ir. Nat.,* **33**: 43.

532 **Logan, W.,** 1943.
Otter taking hooked trout. *Ir. Nat. J.,* **8**: 78.

533 **Longfield, R. E.,** 1928.
A pack of stoats. *Ir. Nat. J.,* **2**: 73.

534 **Lovegrove, R. R., Byrne, E. J. and Rear, D.,** 1965.
Notes on a visit to the Great Skellig Rock, Co. Kerry. *Ir. Nat. J.,* **15**: 47-49. ● Some mammals recorded, including seals.

535 **Lydekker, R.,** 1895.
A Handbook to the British Mammalia. Allen. London.

McAlister, A. and M'Nabb, W. R. (eds.), 1878. See No. 108.

536 **McCalmont, D.,** 1929.
Pine marten in Ireland. *Field,* **153**: 73.

537 **McCartney, G. J.,** 1874.
The red deer of Erris. *Field*, **44**: 31, 116.

538 **McCaughey, W. J. and Fairley, J. S.,** 1969.
Serological reactions to *Brucella* and *Leptospira* in foxes. *Vet. Rec.*, **84**: 542.

539 **McCaughey, W. J. and Fairley, J. S.,** 1971.
Leptospirosis in Irish wildlife. *Vet. Rec.*, **89**: 447. ●
Mostly mice.

540 **McCoy, F.,** 1845.
Contributions to the fauna of Ireland. *Proc. Dubl. nat. Hist. Soc.* in *Ann. Mag. nat. Hist.*, **15**: 270-274.
● Natterer's bat recorded in Ireland.

541 **McEndoo, W.,** 1902.
Notes on the hedgehog. *Ir. Nat.*, **11**: 25.

542 *****MacGillivray, W.,** 1838.
British Quadrupeds. Lizars. Edinburgh.

543 **McIntyre, D.,** 1950.
Habits of the otter. *Field*, **196**: 549. ● Otter swims from Ireland to Scotland.

544 **McLoughlin, J. H.,** 1950.
An otter in Belfast. *Ir. Nat. J.*, **10**: 42.

545 **McMillan, N. F.,** 1945.
The wolf in Ireland. *Ir. Nat. J.*, **8**: 261. ● Some early references.

546 **McMillan, N. F.,** 1971.
More 'last Irish wolves'. *Ir. Nat. J.*, **17**: 103.

547 **M'Skimmin, S.,** 1811.

The History and Antiquities of the County and Town of Carrickfergus. Gordon. Belfast. ● Records whales and seal.

548 **Mackie, J.,** 1953.

Tracking in Co. Antrim. *Ir. Nat. J.,* **11**: 1-3. ● Mammal tracks in snow.

549 **Maguire, S. J.,** 1954.

Some notes on the natural history of Iar-Connacht in the seventeenth century. *Galway Reader,* **4** (2/3): 102-106. ● Wolves.

550 **Mahony, J. A.,** 1877.

On the natural history of Donegal, with some account of its archaeology. *Proc. nat. Hist. Soc. Glasg.,* **3**: 152-166.

551 **Mahony, J. A.,** 1877.

The natural history of Donegal. *Zoologist,* (3) **1**: 290-291.

552 **Malcomson, H. T.,** 1940.

Whale off Co. Antrim coast. *Ir. Nat. J.,* **7**: 297.

553 **Mammal Society of the British Isles,** 1957.

Reports on ringing and returns on grey seals. No. 1. September 1954-August 1956. *Proc. zool. Soc. Lond.,* **128**: 594-596. ● Four recoveries from Ireland.

554 **Marshall, J. D.,** 1835, 1836.

Observations on the zoology of the island of Rathlin, off the northern coast of Ireland. *Phil. Mag.,* (1835)

(3) **7**: 492-493. Also in *Rep. Br. Ass. Advmt Sci.*, (1836) (Dublin: 1835): (Notices and abstracts section) 68-69.

555 **Marshall, J. D., 1836.**
Notes on the Statistics and Natural History of the Island of Rathlin. Hardy. Dublin. ● A species list and a few brief notes.

556 **Mason, T. H., 1936.**
The Islands of Ireland. Batsford. London. ● Mainly rats.

557 **Massy, A. L., 1926.**
Rat in flower garden. *Ir. Nat. J.*, **1**: 115. ● Rat feeding on flower buds.

558 **Matheson, C., 1939.**
A survey of the status of *Rattus rattus* and its subspecies in the sea-ports of Great Britain and Ireland. *J. Anim. Ecol.*, **8**: 76-93.

559 **Maxwell, W. H., 1832.**
Wild Sports of the West. Unwin. London. (Reprinted by the Educational Company of Ireland). ● Deer, otter-hunting, wild-cats. Narrative.

560 **May, G. C., 1924.**
Martens in Co. Limerick. *Ir. Nat.*, **33**: 43.

Meally, V. et al (eds.), 1968. See No. 650.

561 **Meares, C., 1889.**
Hare going to ground. *Field*, **74**: 476.

562 **Metcalfe, H. M.,** 1915.
Marten in Co. Kildare. *Ir. Nat.,* **24**: 218.

563 **Mettam, A. E.,** 1907.
On the presence of a trypanosome in an Irish bat.
Dubl. J. med. Sci., **124**: 417-419.

564 **Middleton, A. D.,** 1929.
The red squirrel in Ireland. *Ir. Nat. J.,* **2**: 149-150.
● Fluctuations in numbers.

565 **Middleton, A. D.,** 1930.
The ecology of the American grey squirrel (*Sciurus carolinensis* Gmelin) in the British Isles. *Proc. zool. Soc. Lond.,* (1930): 808-843. ● Brief reference to spread in Ireland. Includes notes on red squirrels in Ireland.

566 **Middleton, A. D.,** 1931.
The Grey Squirrel. Sidgwick and Jackson. London.
● Little new except a supposed record near Belfast.

567 **Middleton, A. D.,** 1932.
The grey squirrel (*Sciurus carolinensis*) in the British Isles, 1930-32. *J. Anim. Ecol.,* **1**: 166-167.

568 ***Middleton, A. D.,** 1935.
The distribution of the grey squirrel (*Sciurus carolinensis*) in Great Britain in 1935. *J. Anim. Ecol.,* **4**: 274-276. ● Merely confirms continuing presence in Ireland.

569 **Millais, J. G.,** 1897.
British Deer and their Horns. Sotheran. London.

570 **Millais, J. G.,** 1904.
The Mammals of Great Britain and Ireland. Longmans, Green. London. ● A comprehensive account.

571 **Millar, R.,** 1967.
The avifauna of the East Twin, Belfast Harbour and some natural history notes. *Ir. Nat. J.,* **15**: 258-266. ● Some small mammals present and remains of others in pellets of short-eared owl.

572 **Miller, G. S.,** 1912.
Catalogue of the Mammals of Western Europe. British Museum (Natural History). London. ● Includes extensive Irish data, especially for the hare and stoat.

573 **Mitchell, A. T.,** 1929.
The pine marten in Ireland. *Field,* **153**: 73.

574 **Mitchell, G. F.,** 1969.
Pleistocene mammals in Ireland. *Bull. Mammal Soc. Br. Isles,* **31**: 21-25.

575 **Moeran, F. M.,** 1939.
Pine marten in Co. Down. *Ir. Nat. J.,* **7**: 224.

576 **Moffat, C. B.,** 1890.
Habits of the stoat. *Zoologist,* (3) **14**: 380-382.

577 **Moffat, C. B.,** 1892.
The marten in Co. Wexford. *Ir. Nat.,* **1**: 83.

578 **Moffat, C. B.,** 1892.
Marten in Co. Wexford. *Zoologist,* (3) **16**: 263-264.

579 **Moffat, C. B., 1897.**
Irish bats. *Ir. Nat.*, **6**: 135. ● Record of Leisler's bat.

580 **Moffat, C. B., 1898.**
Life and Letters of Alexander Goodman Moore.
Hodges and Figgis. Dublin. ● Several field notes on
mammals unpublished elsewhere and a brief note
on Irish mammals in general, the latter reprinted
from *Guy's South of Ireland Pictorial Guide.* Guy.
Cork. However I have examined two editions of this
tourist guide without seeing it.

581 **Moffat, C. B., 1900.**
The hedgehog and its food. *Ir. Nat.*, **9**: 50.

582 **Moffat, C. B., 1900.**
Hairy-armed bat in Co. Wexford. *Ir. Nat.*, **9**: 162.

583 **Moffat, C. B., 1900.**
The habits of the hairy-armed bat *Vesperugo leisleri*
Kuhl. *Ir. Nat.*, **9**: 235-240.

584 **Moffat, C. B., 1901.**
Breeding habits of the squirrel. *Ir. Nat.*, **10**: 148.

585 **Moffat, C. B., 1902.**
Whiskered bat in Co. Wexford. *Ir. Nat.*, **11**: 103.

586 **Moffat, C. B., 1904.**
Bats, hedgehogs and frogs in winter. *Ir. Nat.*, **13**: 81-
87.

587 **Moffat, C. B., 1905.**
The duration of flight among bats. *Ir. Nat.*, **14**: 97-
108.

588 **Moffat, C. B.,** 1910.
The autumnal mortality among shrews. *Ir. Nat.,* **19**: 121-126.

589 **Moffat, C. B.,** 1911.
Hibernation of Leisler's bat. *Ir. Nat.,* **20**: 115.

590 **Moffat, C. B.,** 1914.
The lesser horse-shoe bat. *Ir. Nat.,* **23**: 153-154.

591 **Moffat, C. B.,** 1916.
Daubenton's bat in Co. Wexford. *Ir. Nat.,* **25**: 171.

592 **Moffat, C. B.,** 1921.
Curious behaviour of a bat. *Ir. Nat.,* **30**: 110-111.

593 **Moffat, C. B.,** 1921.
The breeding of squirrels. *Ir. Nat.,* **30**: 111.

594 **Moffat, C. B.,** 1922.
What bats are common? *Ir. Nat.,* **31**: 12.

595 **Moffat, C. B.,** 1922.
The habits of the long-eared bat. *Ir. Nat.,* **31**: 105-111.

596 **Moffat, C. B.,** 1923.
Is the squirrel a native of Ireland? *Ir. Nat.,* **32**: 33-35.

597 **Moffat, C. B.,** 1923.
Food of the Irish squirrel. *Ir. Nat.,* **32**: 77-82.

598 **Moffat, C. B.,** 1926.
The hedgehog. *Ir. Nat. J.,* **1**: 45-46. ● Notes.

599 **Moffat, C. B., 1926.**
The lesser or pygmy shrew. *Ir. Nat. J.*, **1**: 66-68. ●
Notes.

600 **Moffat, C. B., 1926.**
The badger. *Ir. Nat. J.*, **1**: 130-132. ● Notes.

601 **Moffat, C. B., 1926.**
The Irish stoat. *Ir. Nat. J.*, **1**: 150-151. ● Notes.

602 **Moffat, C. B., 1927.**
The pine marten. *Ir. Nat. J.*, **1**: 170-171. ● Notes.

603 **Moffat, C. B., 1927.**
The otter. *Ir. Nat. J.*, **1**: 209-212. ● Notes.

604 **Moffat, C. B., 1927.**
The fox. *Ir. Nat. J.*, **1**: 231-233. ● Notes.

605 **Moffat, C. B., 1927.**
The squirrel. *Ir. Nat. J.*, **1**: 250-252. ● Notes on the
red squirrel.

606 **Moffat, C. B., 1927.**
The Irish hare. *Ir. Nat. J.*, **1**: 271-273. ● Notes.

607 **Moffat, C. B., 1928.**
The rabbit. *Ir. Nat. J.*, **2**: 28-30. ● Notes.

608 **Moffat, C. B., 1928.**
The black rat. *Ir. Nat. J.*, **2**: 47-49. ● Notes.

609 **Moffat, C. B., 1928.**
The hare in the Isle of Man. *Ir. Nat. J.*, **2**: 64. ● See
also No. 326.

610 **Moffat, C. B.,** 1928.
The brown rat. *Ir. Nat. J.,* **2**: 87-89. ● Notes.

611 **Moffat, C. B.,** 1928.
The field mouse. *Ir. Nat. J.,* **2**: 106-109. ● Notes.

612 **Moffat, C. B.,** 1929.
The house mouse. *Ir. Nat. J.,* **2**: 195-197. ● Notes.

613 **Moffat, C. B.,** 1930.
The pipistrelle. *Ir. Nat. J.,* **3**: 26-29. ● Notes.

614 **Moffat, C. B.,** 1930.
The hairy-armed bat. *Ir. Nat. J.,* **3**: 50-54. ● Notes.

615 **Moffat, C. B.,** 1931.
The long-eared bat. *Ir. Nat. J.,* **3**: 182-185. ● Notes.

616 **Moffat, C. B.,** 1932.
Daubenton's bat. *Ir. Nat. J.,* **4**: 26-28. ● Notes.

617 **Moffat, C. B.,** 1932.
The whiskered bat. *Ir. Nat. J.,* **4**: 106-109. ● Notes.

618 **Moffat, C. B.,** 1938.
The mammals of Ireland. *Proc. R. Ir. Acad.,* **44**B: 61-128. ● An extremely comprehensive paper.

619 **Moffat, C. B. and Pack-Beresford, H. D.,** 1939.
Killing of ornamental fowl at Powerscourt, Co. Wicklow. Heron or otter? *Ir. Nat. J.,* **7**: 216-217. ● Correspondence.

620 **Molyneux, T.,** 1697, 1755.

A discourse concerning the large horns frequently found under ground in Ireland, concluding from them that the great American deer, call'd a moose, was formerly common in Ireland: with remarks on other things natural to that country. *Phil. Trans. R. Soc.,* **19**: 509-512. Also in Boate, G., Molyneux, T. *et al.* 1755. *A Natural History of Ireland, in Three Parts.* Ewing. Dublin. (There may be earlier editions). ● Cetacea.

621 **Montgomery, F. J.,** 1907.

Winter whitening of the Irish hare. *Field,* **109**: 445.

622 **Mooney, O. V.,** 1952.

Irish deer and forest relations. *Ir. For.,* **9**: 11-27.

623 **Moore, R. St. L.,** 1909.

Black rats in Ireland. *Field,* **114**: 464.

624 **More, A. G.,** 1878.

White-nosed dolphin on the Irish coast. *Zoologist,* (3) **2**: 292.

625 **More, A. G.,** 1891.

Irish localities for Natterer's bat. *Zoologist,* (3) **15**: 304-305.

626 **Moriarty, C.,** 1955.

Behaviour of hares on mud flats. *Ir. Nat. J.,* **11**: 310.

627 **Moriarty, C.,** 1961.

Pine marten, *Martes martes* (L.), in Co. Wicklow. *Ir. Nat. J.,* **13**: 239.

628 **Moryson, F., 1735.**
The Description of Ireland. Powell. Dublin. ● Includes references to deer, wolves and a few other records.

629 **Mulloy, F., 1970.**
A note on the occurrence of deer in Ireland. *Deer,* **2**: 502-504.

630 **Murray, H. B., 1871.**
Squirrels and oak-galls. *Field,* **38**: 301.

631 **'Nahanik', 1891.**
Irish hares. *Land. Wat.,* **51**: 311. ● Possible interbreeding between imported hares and Irish hares.

632 **'Nahanik', 1893.**
Hares. *Land. Wat.,* **55**: 195. ● Possible introductions.

633 **Neale, E., 1948.**
The Badger. Collins. London. ● Note and map of possible distribution in Ireland.

634 **Neal, M. and Rankin, D. H., 1941.**
Breeding of the common seal in Strangford Lough. *Ir. Nat. J.,* **7**: 320.

635 **N. H., 1831.**
Birds at and near Londonderry. *Mag. nat. Hist.,* **4**: 269-270. ● Includes a brief list of mammals.

636 **Nuttall, G. H. F., Warburton, C., Cooper, W. F. and Robinson, L. E., 1908.**
Ticks. A Monograph of the Ixoidea. University Press.

Cambridge. ● A few records from Irish wild mammals.

637 **O'Connell, H., 1893.**
Breeding of the squirrel (*Sciurus vulgaris*), and otter (*Lutra vulgaris*). *Ir. Nat.*, **2**: 56.

638 **O'Connell, J. H., 1900.**
The hedgehog and its food. *Ir. Nat.*, **9**: 50.

639 **Odlum, W. P., 1955.**
Two bats hitherto unrecorded in Co. Leix. *Ir. Nat. J.*, **11**: 310. ● Pipistrelle and Leisler's bat.

640 **O'Flaherty, R., [1684] 1846.**
A Chorographical Description of West or H'Ir Connaught. Irish Archaeological Society. Dublin. (Original manuscript 1684). ● Detailed list of mammals in mid-west of Ireland with notes.

641 ***O'Gorman, F., 1963.**
The breeding status of the grey seal in Ireland. *Bull. Mammal Soc. Br. Isles*, **20**: 15-16. ● A summary of available data.

642 **O'Gorman, F., 1965.**
Irish deer as a valuable natural resource. *Ann. Rep. Game Coun. Ire.*, (1965): 71-75.

643 **O'Gorman, F., 1965.**
The bank vole in Ireland. *Bull. Mammal Soc. Br. Isles*, **24**: 5-6.

644 **O'Gorman, F., 1965.**
Argas vespertilionis (Latreille), a tick previously un-

recorded in Ireland. *Ir. Nat. J.*, **15**: 19. ● From pipistrelle bats.

645 **O'Gorman, F., 1965.**

Ischnopsyllus octactenus (Kolenati) (Siphonaptera,
Ischnopsyllidae) a bat flea from mid County Cork.
Ir. Nat. J., **15**: 107-108.

646 **O'Gorman, F., 1965.**

Does the long-eared bat, *Plecotus austriachus*
(Fisher) occur in Ireland? *Ir. Nat. J.*, **15**: 109. ● An
appeal for specimens. A search of Irish museum collections for *P. austriachus* produced none.

647 **O'Gorman, F., 1965.**

Second record of Natterer's bat, *Myotis nattereri*
(Kuhl) in Co. Cork. *Ir. Nat. J.*, **15**: 111.

648 **O'Gorman, F., 1965.**

Mammals of Tory Island, Co. Donegal, Ireland. *Proc.
zool. Soc. Lond.*, **145**: 155-158.

649 **O'Gorman, F., 1967.**

Some aspects of deer ecology in Killarney, County
Kerry. *Bull. Mammal Soc. Br. Isles*, **28**: 9-10.

650 **O'Gorman, F. (in Meally, V. et al [eds.]). 1968.**

Encyclopedia of Ireland. Figgis. Dublin. ● Notes on
Irish mammals.

651 **O'Gorman, F. and Claassens, A. J. M., 1965.**

Sex ratios of fleas from Irish bats. *Entomologist's
Gaz.*, **16**: 20-24.

652 **O'Gorman, F. and Claassens, A. J. M., 1965.**
Myotis nattereri (Kuhl), a bat new to Co. Kerry. *Ir. Nat. J.*, **15**: 53-54.

653 **O'Gorman, F. and Claassens, A. J. M., 1965.**
Siphonaptera new to Co. Kilkenny. *Ir. Nat. J.*, **15**: 69-72. ● Fleas from bats.

654 **O'Gorman, F. and Claassens, A. J. M., 1965.**
The second record of *Ischnopsyllus* (*Ischnopsyllus*) *simplex simplex* Rothschild 1906 (Siphonaptera) in Ireland. *Ir. Nat. J.*, **15**: 75-76. ● Flea from Natterer's bat.

655 **O'Gorman, F. and Fairley, J. S., 1965.**
A colony of *Plecotus auritus* from Co. Kilkenny. *Proc. zool. Soc. Lond.*, **145**: 154-155. ● Includes body measurements.

656 **Ogilby, J. D., 1872.**
Weasel in Ireland. *Field*, **39**: 234. ● Supposed records.

657 **Ogilby, J. D., 1874.**
The Irish hare. *Field*, **44**: 116. ● Winter whitening.

658 **Ogilby, J. D., 1874.**
Hairy-armed bat in County Dublin. *Zoologist*, (2) **9**: 4246.

659 **Ogilby, J. D., 1876.**
Occurrence of the whitesided dolphin on the Irish coast. *Zoologist*, (2) **11**: 5077-5078.

660 **Ogilby, J. D.,** 1877.
Natural history of Donegal. *Zoologist,* (3) **1**: 223-224.

661 **Ogilby, R. L.,** 1843.
(Exhibit of white variety of the Irish hare). *Proc. zool. Soc. Lond.,* (1843): 75. ● Exhibit only.

662 **Ogilby, W.,** 1834.
Notice of a new species of the otter from the north of Ireland. *Proc. zool. Soc. Lond.,* (1843): 110-111.

O'Hanlon, J. and O'Leary, E., 1907. See No. 791.

663 **O'Mahony, E.,** 1931.
Notes on the mammals of the North Bull, Dublin Bay. *Ir. Nat. J.,* **3**: 199-201.

664 **O'Mahony, E.,** 1935.
Discovery of a second race of house-mouse in Ireland. *Ir. Nat. J.,* **5**: 218-219. ● *Mus musculus orientalis* stated to be present in Ireland.

665 **O'Mahoney, E.,** 1935.
The North Bull house mouse. *Ir. Nat. J.,* **5**: 291.

666 **O'Mahony, E.,** 1937.
On some forms of the house mouse *Mus musculus* Linn. in Ireland. *Ir. Nat. J.,* **6**: 288-290. ● Three races described.

667 **O'Mahony, E.,** 1939.
A preliminary list of Irish fleas. *Entomologist's mon. Mag.,* **75**: 124-126.

668 **O'Mahony, E., 1939.**
Notes on the Irish Siphonaptera I. *Entomologist's mon. Mag.*, **75**: 253-254.

669 **O'Mahony, E., 1940.**
Notes on Irish Siphonaptera II. *Entomologist's mon. Mag.*, **76**: 205.

670 **O'Mahony, E., 1941.**
Notes on Irish Siphonaptera III. *Entomologist's mon. Mag.*, **77**: 208.

671 **O'Mahony, E., 1941.**
Notes on Irish Siphonaptera IV. *Entomologist's mon. Mag.*, **77**: 231.

672 **O'Mahony, E., 1942.**
Notes on Irish Siphonaptera V. *Entomologist's mon. Mag.*, **78**: 199.

673 **O'Mahony, E., 1944.**
A note on some Irish Anoplura Siphunculata. *Entomologist's mon. Mag.*, **80**: 5.

674 **O'Mahony, E., 1945.**
A scarce Irish beetle *Leptinus testaceus* Müll (Col. Leptinidae). *Entomologist's mon. Mag.*, **81**: 6. ● From fieldmouse nest.

675 **O'Mahony, E., 1946.**
Trichodectes vulpis Denny (Mallophaga) in Ireland. *Entomologist's mon. Mag.*, **82**: 160. ● From foxes.

676 **O'Mahony, E., 1946.**
Records of Trichodectidae (Mallophaga). *Entomologist's mon. Mag.*, **82**: 211.

677 **O'Mahony, E., 1946.**
Records of Anoplura. *Entomologist's mon. Mag.*, **82**: 231. ● Only Irish material from rabbit.

678 **O'Mahony, E., 1947.**
Leptinus testaceus Müll. An additional Irish record. *Entomologist's mon. Mag.*, **83**: 190. ● From field-mouse.

679 **O'Mahony, E., 1947.**
The mammal ectoparasites of the North Bull Island, Dublin Bay. *Ir. Nat. J.*, **9**: 78-79. ● Fleas, lice.

680 **O'Mahony, E., 1948.**
Some miscellaneous Siphonaptera. *Entomologist's mon. Mag.*, **84**: 89.

681 **O'Mahony, E., 1949.**
The fleas of the North Bull Island, Dublin Bay. *Entomologist's mon. Mag.*, **85**: 139-140.

682 **O'Riordan, C. E., 1969.**
Recent strandings on the Irish coast. *Ir. Nat. J.*, **16**: 206. ● Record of sperm whale stranding.

683 **O'Rourke, D. V. W., 1956.**
Pine marten in Co. Mayo. *Field*, **208**: 692.

684 **O'Rourke, F. J., 1964.**
Ischnopsyllus intermedius (Rothschild), a bat flea new to Co. Cork. *Ir. Nat. J.*, **14**: 315-316.

685 **O'Rourke, F. J.,** 1970.
   The Fauna of Ireland. An Introduction to the Land Vertebrates. Mercier. Cork. ● Includes a useful review of the mammals, the most modern available.

686 **Orr. H. L.,** 1899-1900.
   The hedgehog and its food. *Ir. Nat.,* **8**: 268; **9**: 110.

687 **Orr, H. L.,** 1901.
   Winter flight of bats. *Ir. Nat.,* **10**: 51.

688 **Otway, A. L.,** 1901.
   Irish red deer. *Ir. Nat.,* **10**: 101-104.

689 **Otway, S. G.,** 1840.
   Remarkable change of habitat in the hare. *Ann. nat. Hist.,* **5**: 362-363.

690 **Pack-Beresford, D. R.,** 1900.
   The Irish rat *Mus hibernicus. Ir. Nat.,* **9**: 110.

691 **Pack-Beresford, D. R.,** 1905.
   Natterer's bat in Co. Carlow. *Ir. Nat.,* **14**: 248.

692 **Pack-Beresford, D. R.,** 1906.
   Whiskered bat in Co. Carlow. *Ir. Nat.,* **15**: 16.

693 **Pack-Beresford, D. R.,** 1906.
   Vesperugo leisleri in Co. Carlow. *Ir. Nat.,* **15**: 194.

694 ***Pack-Beresford, D. R.,** 1920.
   The marten in Ireland. *Ir. Nat.,* **29**: 107. ● Review of earlier records in *Ir. Nat.* References not given.

695 **Pack-Beresford, H. D.,** 1936.
Cat kills stoat and stoat kills carrier pigeon. *Ir. Nat., J.,* **6**: 146.

696 **Pack-Beresford, H. D.,** 1939.
Rat and kittens. *Ir. Nat. J.,* **7**: 224. ● Anecdotal.

697 **Pack-Beresford, R.,** 1928.
Hares going to ground. *Ir. Nat. J.,* **2**: 104, 111.

698 ***Page, F. J. T.,** 1962.
Fallow Deer. Sunday Times Publications. London. (Animals of Britain No. 11).

699 ***Page, F. J. T.,** 1962.
Red Deer. Sunday Times Publications. London. (Animals of Britain No. 13).

700 **Page, F. J. T.,** 1971.
Field Guide to British Deer (Second edition). Mammal Society. ● Distribution in Ireland summarised.

701 **Page, R. J.,** 1967.
A tick new to Ireland—*Ixodes trianguliceps* Birula 1895. *Entomologist's mon. Mag.,* **103**: 120-122. ● From fieldmouse.

702 **P. A. K.,** 1883.
Black rat in Co. Wexford. *Field,* **62**: 735.

703 **Palmer, R. F. and Skillen, S.,** 1962.
Fleas from Irish bats. *Ir. Nat. J.,* **14**: 78.

704 **Pantelouris, E. M. and Arnason, A., 1967.**
Serum proteins of *Apodemus sylvaticus* and *Mus musculus*. *Comp. Biochem. Physiol.*, **21**: 533-539. ● Irish wild *Apodemus* used.

705 **Passingham, G. H., 1895.**
Rat and hedgehog. *Field*, **86**: 903. ● Heresay. Hedgehog kills rat.

706 **Patten, C. J., 1908.**
Rambles on Achill Island. *Ir. Nat.*, **17**: 189-203.

707 **Patterson, R., 1858, 1859.**
Note on the occurrence of *Hyperoodon butzkopf* (bottle-nosed whale). *Proc. Dubl. Univ. zool. bot. Ass.*, (1859) **1**: 4-6. Also in *Nat. Hist. Rev.*, (Proceedings of the Societies section) (1858) **5**: 49-50.

708 **Patterson, R., 1886.**
A recent visit to Tory Island. *Proc. Rep. Belf. nat. Hist. phil. Soc.*, (1885-86): 27-30. ● Rabbit and 'common mouse' only mammals recorded.

709 **Patterson, R., 1887.**
Some account of the whale and seal fisheries, past and present. *Proc. Rep. Belf. nat. Hist. phil. Soc.*, (1886-87): 112-114. ● Only item of interest is a record of a white-beaked dolphin.

710 **Patterson, R., 1894.**
Notes on the occurrences of the marten (*Martes sylvatica*) in Ulster. *Ir. Nat.*, **3**: 106-109.

711 **Patterson, R., 1894.**
The occurrence of the marten (*Martes sylvatica*) in

Ulster. *Proc. Rep. Belf. nat. Hist. phil. Soc.*, (1893-94): 76. ● Two records.

712 **Patterson, R.,** 1900.
Whiskered bat in Co. Down. *Ir. Nat.*, **9**: 162.

713 **Patterson, R.,** 1900.
Martens in the north of Ireland. *Ir. Nat.*, **9**: 162.

714 **Patterson, R.,** 1900.
Marten in Co. Londonderry. *Ir. Nat.*, **9**: 186.

715 **Patterson, R.,** 1900.
Bats in the north of Ireland. *Ir. Nat.*, **9**: 233.

716 **Patterson, R.,** 1900.
Natterer's bat in Co. Antrim. *Ir. Nat.*, **9**: 274.

717 **Patterson, R.,** 1900.
The disappearance of the fox from Co. Antrim. *Ir. Nat.*, **9**: 275-277.

718 **Patterson, R.,** 1901.
Foxes in Co. Donegal. *Ir. Nat.*, **10**: 231-232.

719 **Patterson, R.,** 1901.
Notes on the hedgehog. *Ir. Nat.*, **10**: 254.

720 **Patterson, R.,** 1903.
Marten in Co. Londonderry. *Ir. Nat.*, **12**: 139.

721 **Patterson, R.,** 1903.
The hairy-armed bat. *Ir. Nat.*, **12**: 320. ● New records.

722   **Patterson, R., 1905.**
Hairy-armed bat in Down and Antrim. *Ir. Nat.,* **14**: 20.

723   **Patterson, R., 1908.**
Ulster Nature Notes. Mullan. Belfast. ● Notes on bats, badgers, stoats, wolves and an analysis of barn owl pellets.

724   **Patterson, R. and Foster, N. H., 1904.**
Irish Field Club Union report of the fourth triennial conference and excursion, held at Sligo, July 12th to 18th, 1904. II Zoology. Vetebrata. *Ir. Nat.,* **13**: 182-183. ● Some species recorded in the locality.

725   **Patterson, R. and Foster, N. H., 1907.**
Irish Field Club Union. Report of the fifth triennial conference and excursion, held at Cork, July 11th to 16th, 1907. Vertebrata. *Ir. Nat.,* **16**: 269-272. ● A few species recorded in the locality.

726   **Patterson, R. L., 1877.**
Some notes on the Cetacea occasionally visiting Belfast Lough. *Proc. Rep. Belf. nat. Hist. phil. Soc.,* (1876-77): 53-59.

727   **Patterson, R. L., 1880.**
Birds, Fishes and Cetacea Commonly Frequenting Belfast Lough. Ward. Belfast. Bogue. London.

728   **Patterson, R. L., 1883.**
Occurrence of white-beaked dolphin in Ireland. *Field,* **61**: 605.

729   **Patterson, R. L., 1899.**
Irish bats. *Ir. Nat.,* **8**: 61. ● Appearance of bats after hibernation.

730　**Patterson, R. L.,** 1900.
Notes on the Irish Cetacea. *Ir. Nat.,* **9**: 210-212.

731　**Patterson, R. L.,** 1900.
The vision of whales. *Ir. Nat.,* **9**: 273.

732　**Patterson, R. L.,** 1901.
Common dolphin in Belfast Lough. *Ir. Nat.,* **10**: 74.

733　**Patterson, R. M.,** 1926.
A stoat's mid-day meal. *Ir. Nat. J.,* **1**: 70. ● Includes rabbits.

734　**Payne-Gallwey, R.,** 1882.
The Fowler in Ireland. Van Voorst. London. ● General, especially deer.

735　***Pease, A. E.,** 1898.
The Badger. Lawrence and Bullen. London. ● Reprints correspondence in the *Field* on Irish badgers.

736　**Pentland, G. H.,** 1896.
Marten in Co. Limerick. *Zoologist,* (3) **20**: 17.

737　**Pentland, G. H.,** 1902.
Strange conduct of a badger. *Ir. Nat.,* **11**: 24.

738　**Pentland, G. H.,** 1912.
Notes on the increase and decrease of some mammals, birds and insects in the County of Louth during the last fifty years. *Ir. Nat.,* **21**: 145-148.

739　**Pentland, G. H.,** 1915.
Dolphins in the Boyne. *Ir. Nat.,* **24**: 76.

740 **Pentland, G. H.,** 1915.
Disappearance of squirrels. *Ir. Nat.*, **24**: 76.

741 **Pentland, G. H.,** 1917.
Speed of flight of Leisler's bat. *Ir. Nat.*, **26**: 19.

742 **Pentland, G. H.,** 1917.
Boldness of a stoat. *Ir. Nat.*, **26**: 20.

743 **Pentland, G. H.,** 1917.
Badgers and hedgehogs. *Ir. Nat.*, **26**: 20. ● Possible
instance of badgers reducing numbers of hedgehogs.

744 **Pentland, G. H.,** 1920.
Unusual capture of a seal. *Ir. Nat.*, **29**: 79-80. ● Seal
takes fishing bait.

745 **Pentland, G. H.,** 1920.
Pine marten in Co. Louth. *Ir. Nat.*, **29**: 80, 124.

746 **Persse, H.,** 1900.
Sheep attacked by fallow buck. *Field*, **95**: 579.

747 **Pomeroy, J. (in Harvie-Brown, J. A. and Buckley, T. E.),**
1892.
*A Vertebrate Fauna of Argyll and the Innter Heb-
rides*. Douglas. Edinburgh. ● Weights and winter
whitening of Irish hares.

748 **Portsmouth, Lord,** 1901.
Weight of Irish deer. *Field*, **98**: 601.

749 **Powerscourt, Lord,** 1937.
Dog friendly with a fox. *Ir. Nat. J.*, **6**: 252.

750 **Powerscourt, Viscount,** 1884.

The acclimatization of Japanese deer at Powerscourt. *Proc. zool. Soc. Lond.,* (1884): 207-209.

751 **Praeger, R. L. (in Fletcher, G. [ed.]),** 1921-22.

The Provinces of Ireland. University Press. Cambridge. ● Brief notes on the mammals of each province. Little new.

752 ***Praeger, R. L.,** 1950.

The Natural History of Ireland. Collins. London. ● Includes a general account of the mammals.

753 **Pycraft, W. P.,** 1914.

Sowerby's whale off Co. Wexford. *Field,* **124**: 664. ● Stranding. See also page 726 of same volume.

754 **R. A. A.,** 1891.

Hare frequenting a burrow. *Field,* **78**: 88.

755 **R. C.,** 1916.

Wild life on Achill Island. *Field,* **127**: 364. ● Foxes cross to Achill Island.

756 **Redahan, E.,** 1967.

A search for *Trichinella spiralis* in pigs and rats in Ireland. *Ir. Vet. J.,* **21**: 168-170. ● Results negative.

Reeves, W., 1861. See No. 47.

757 **Robinson, W. G.,** 1897.

Food of the squirrel. *Field,* **89**: 970. ● Brief (heresay) reference to damage to trees.

758 **Rogers, A. R.,** 1959.
Pine marten *Martes martes martes* (L.) in Co. Down woods. *Ir. Nat. J.,* **13**: 42.

759 **Rohu and Sons,** 1927.
Black seal on the south coast. *Ir. Nat. J.,* **1**: 195.

760 **Rohu and Sons,** 1927.
The pine marten. *Ir. Nat. J.,* **1**: 207-208.

761 **Ross, J. G. and Fairley, J. S.,** 1969.
Studies of disease in the red fox (*Vulpes vulpes*) in Northern Ireland. *J. Zool., Lond.,* **157**: 375-381. ● Includes ectoparasites and endoparasites.

762 **Rothschild, N. C.,** 1899.
Irish fleas. *Ir. Nat.,* **8**: 266.

763 **Ruttledge, R. F.,** 1920.
The pine marten in Ireland. *Ir. Nat.,* **29**: 125-127.

764 **Ruttledge, R. F.,** 1924.
Note on the distribution of the squirrel in Ireland. *Ir. Nat.,* **33**: 73-74.

765 **Ruttledge, R. F.,** 1943.
Lesser horse-shoe bat (*Rhinolophus hipposideros*) in Co. Mayo. *Ir. Nat. J.,* **8**: 77.

766 **Ruttledge, R. F.,** 1945.
Occurrences of the lesser horseshoe bat (*Rhinolophus hipposideros*) in Co. Mayo. *Ir. Nat. J.,* **8**: 261.

767 **Ruttledge, R. F.,** 1948.
Pine marten in Co. Donegal. *Ir. Nat. J.,* **9**: 215-216.

768 **Ruttledge, R. F.,** 1949.
Leisler's bat in Co. Mayo. *Ir. Nat. J.,* **9**: 307-308.

769 **Ruttledge, R. F.,** 1951.
Rats eating hawthorn berries. *Ir. Nat. J.,* **10**: 217.

770 **Ruttledge, R. F.,** 1952.
Daubenton's bat in Co. Mayo. *Ir. Nat. J.,* **10**: 274. ●
Identification of an individual in flight.

771 **Ruttledge, R. F.,** 1955.
Leisler's bat in Co. Kilkenny. *Ir. Nat. J.,* **11**: 310.

772 **Ruttledge, R. F.,** 1961.
Leisler's bat, *Nyctalus leisleri* in Co. Kildare. *Ir. Nat.
J.,* **13**: 276.

773 **Ruttledge, R. F.,** 1966.
Ireland's Birds. Witherby. London. ● Sole point of
interest is decline in buzzards after reduction of
rabbit numbers by myxomatosis.

774 **Rutty, J.,** 1772.
*An Essay towards a Natural History of the County
of Dublin.* Sleator. Dublin. ● Includes notes on wild
mammals. Some of these are accurate and of some
interest.

775 **Sampson, G. V.,** 1802.
Statistical Survey of the County of Londonderry.
Graisberry and Campbell. Dublin. ● Brief notes on
rabbit warrens and marine mammals.

776 **Savage, R. J. G.,** 1966.
Irish Pleistocene mammals. *Ir. Nat. J.,* **15**: 117-130.
● The most modern and thorough account.

777 **Scharff, R. F.,** 1894.
On the origin of the Irish land and freshwater fauna. *Proc. R. Ir. Acad.,* (3) **3**: 479-485.

778 **Scharff, R. F.,** 1895.
Irish hare turning white in winter. *Zoologist,* (3) **19**: 149-150.

779 **Scharff, R. F.,** 1896.
Canis vulpes melanogaster Bonap. in Ireland. *Ir. Nat. J.,* **5**: 178.

780 **Scharff, R. F.,** 1897.
On the origin of the European fauna. *Proc. R. Ir. Acad.,* (3) **4**: 427-514.

781 **Scharff, R. F.,** 1898.
The harvest mouse. *Ir. Nat.,* **7**: 125. ● Comment on No. 137.

782 **Scharff, R. F.,** 1898.
The English hare in Ireland. *Ir. Nat.,* **7**: 126.

783 **Scharff, R. F.,** 1899.
The History of the European Fauna. Scott. London.

784 **Scharff, R. F.,** 1900.
A list of the Irish Cetacea. *Ir. Nat.,* **9**: 83-91.

785 **Scharff, R. F.,** 1902.
A white-beaked dolphin (*Lagenorhynchus albiros-tris*) in Dublin Bay. *Ir. Nat.,* **11**: 66-67.

786 **Scharff, R. F.,** 1902.
Lesser horse-shoe bat in Co. Clare. *Ir. Nat.,* **11**: 175.

787   **Scharff, R. F., 1905.**
       The wild cat in Ireland. *Ir. Nat.,* **14**: 79, 184.

788   **Scharff, R. F., 1905.**
       Bottle-nosed dolphins in Dublin Bay. *Ir. Nat.,* **14**: 121-122.

789   **Scharff, R. F., 1906.**
       On the former occurrence of the African wild cat in Ireland. *Proc. R. Ir. Acad.,* **26**B: 1-12.

790   **Scharff, R. F., 1907.**
       European Animals: Their Geological History and Geograph'cal Distribution. Constable. London. ● Comparatively little on Irish mammals.

791   **Scharff, R. F. (in O'Hanlon, J. and O'Leary, E.), 1907.**
       History of Queen's County. Sealy, Bryers and Walker. Dublin. ● Brief notes on the mammals. Little original.

792   **Scharff, R. F., 1909.**
       On the occurrence of a speckled otter in Ireland. *Ir. Nat.,* **18**: 141-142.

793   **Scharff, R. F., 1909.**
       Irish stoat with nine young. *Ir. Nat.,* **18**: 160.

794   **Scharff, R. F., 1910-11.**
       The Irish whale fishery. *Ir. Nat.,* **19**: 229-233; **20**: 141.

795   **Scharff, R. F., 1911.**
       Some notes on Irish seals. *Ir. Nat.,* **20**: 41-44.

796   **Scharff, R. F., 1911.**
       The ringed seal in Irish waters. *Ir. Nat.,* **20**: 80.

797 **Scharff, R. F.,** 1913.
The supposed former occurrence of the wild cat in Ireland. *Ir. Nat.,* **22**: 84.

798 **Scharff, R. F.,** 1913.
On the supposed occurrence of the wild cat in Ireland. *Ir. Nat.,* **22**: 127-128.

799 **Scharff, R. F.,** 1915.
On the Irish names of mammals. *Ir. Nat.,* **24**: 45-53.

800 **Scharff, R. F.,** 1915.
A beaked whale on the Wexford coast. *Ir. Nat.,* **24**: 64.

801 **Scharff, R. F.,** 1915.
The speckled otter. *Ir. Nat.,* **24**: 76.

802 **Scharff, R. F.,** 1916.
Cuvier's whale in Irish waters. *Ir. Nat.,* **25**: 68.

803 **Scharff, R. F.,** 1918.
The Irish red deer. *Ir. Nat.,* **27**: 133-139.

804 **Scharff, R. F.,** 1919-20.
A new Irish whale. *Ir. Nat.,* **28**: 130-131; **29**: 27.

805 **Scharff, R. F.,** 1920.
The hooded or bladder-nosed seal, *Cystophora cristata* (Erxl.). *Ir. Nat.,* **29**: 93-94.

806 **Scharff, R. F.,** 1922.
Is the squirrel a native Irish species? *Ir. Nat.,* **31**: 51-54.

807 **Scharff, R. F., 1922.**
     The wolf in Ireland. *Ir. Nat.,* **31**: 133-136.

808 **Scharff, R. F., 1923.**
     The squirrel in Ireland. *Ir. Nat.,* **32**: 63.

809 **Scharff, R. F., 1924.**
     The wolf in Ireland. *Ir. Nat.,* **33**: 95.

810 **Schwarz, E. and Schwarz, H. K., 1943.**
     The wild and commersal stocks of the house mouse, *Mus musculus* Linnaeus. *J. Mammal.,* **24**: 59-72. ● Comments on alleged subspecies in Nos. 664 and 666.

811 **Sclater, J., 1875.**
     Hobby preying on bats. *Zoologist,* (2) **10**: 4537. ● Bat remains in gut.

812 **Sclater, P. L., 1897.**
     Note on the Irish otter. *Proc. zool. Soc. Lond.,* (1897): 311.

813 **Scott, A., 1960.**
     A bottle-nosed dolphin *Tursiops truncatus* on Co. Antrim shore. *Ir. Nat. J.,* **13**: 183-184, 240.

814 **Scott, R., 1864, 1865.**
     Catalogue of the mammalian fossils which have been hitherto discovered in Ireland. *J. geol. Soc. Dubl.,* (1864) 10: 143-151. Also in *Dubl. Q. Jl. Sci.,* (1865) **5**: 49-56. ● Wolves, whales.

815 **Scouler, J., 1833.**
     Notice of animals which have disappeared from Ire-

land during the period of authentic history. *J. geol. Soc. Dubl.*, **1**: 224-231. ● Deer, martens, wolves. Brief notes on early bounties on other species.

816 **Sharrock, J. T. R.,** 1967-68.
Cetacea off Cape Clear Island. *Cape Clear Isl. Bird Obs. Rep.*, **8**: 42-44; **9**: 53-55.

817 **Sharrock, J. T. R.,** 1969.
Mammals at Cape Clear Island in 1968. *Cape Clear Isl. Bird Obs. Rep.*, **10**: 24-25.

818 **Sharrock, J. T. R., Fogden, M. P. L., Fogden, S. C. L., Kinnear, P. K. and Simms, C.,** 1968.
The mammals of Cape Clear Island, 1959-67. *Cape Clear Isl. Bird Obs. Rep.*, **9**: 51-52.

819 **Sheals, A.,** 1921.
The breeding of squirrels. *Ir. Nat.*, **30**: 111.

820 **Shorten, M.,** 1954.
Squirrels. Collins. London.

821 *****Shorten, M.,** 1954.
Grey Squirrels. Sunday Times Publications. London (Animals of Britain No. 5).

822 *****Shorten, M.,** 1962.
Squirrels. *Bull. Minist. Agric. Fish Fd, Lond.*, **184**: 1-42.

823 **Simpson, M. J.,** 1895.
Hedgehogs in captivity. *Ir. Nat.*, **4**: 136.

824 **'Sixty-one', 1875.**
A very bold otter. *Field,* **46**: 477. ● Otter takes bait on fishing line.

825 **Skillen, J., 1927.**
The otter. *Ir. Nat. J.,* **1**: 248. ● Correspondence on scarcity of otters in Co. Antrim.

826 **Skillen, S., 1959.**
Irish bats. *Ir. Nat. J.,* **13**: 66-69. ● New records, notes and a key.

827 **Skillen, S., 1960.**
Barn-owl attacking hare. *Ir. Nat. J.,* **13**: 189.

828 **Smit, F. G. A. M., 1955.**
Two new subspecies of fleas (Siphonaptera) from the British Isles. *Trans. R. ent. Soc. Lond.,* **107**: 341-356. ● From fieldmice.

829 **Smit, F. G. A. M., 1956.**
Preliminary description of two new European fleas. *Entomologist's mon. Mag.,* **92**: 296.

830 **Smit, F. G. A. M., 1957.**
Handbooks for the Identification of British Insects. Siphonaptera. (**1**[16]). Royal Entomological Society of London. London. ● Includes distribution of Irish fleas.

831 **Smit, F. G. A. M., 1957.**
The recorded distribution and hosts of Siphonaptera in Britain. *Entomologist's Gaz.,* **8**: 45-75. ● Includes Ireland.

832 **Smith, C.,** 1750.

The Antient and Present State of the County and City of Cork. Privately published. Dublin. ● Brief references to Cetacea, deer parks and hares.

833 **Smith, C.,** 1756.

The Antient and Present State of the County of Kerry. Privately published. Dublin. ● Brief references to deer, seals and rabbits.

834 **Smith, C.,** 1774.

The Ancient and Present State of the County and City of Waterford. Privately published. Dublin. ● Brief references to Cetacea, deer, hares and seals.

835 ***Smith, E. A.,** 1966.

A review of the world's grey seal population. *J. Zool., Lond.,* **150**: 463-489. ● Brief review of Irish information and distribution map.

836 **Smith, O.,** 1893.

Squirrels in Ireland. *Ir. Nat.,* **2**: 324. ● Increase in numbers.

837 **Smith, R. W.,** 1856, 1858.

(On a disease of the foot bones of the red deer). *Proc. Dubl. nat. Hist. Soc.,* (1858) **1**: 12. Also in *Nat. Hist. Rev.,* (Proceedings of the Societies section) (1856) **3**: 52.

838 **'Snaffle',** 1904.

The Roedeer. Harwar. London.

839 ***Southwell, T.,** 1881.

Seals and Whales of the British Seas. Jarrold. London. ● Little on Ireland.

840 **Southwell, T.,** 1889.

The so-called *Mus hibernicus. Zoologist,* (3) **13**: 321-323.

841 ***Southern, H. N. (ed.),** 1964.

The Handbook of British Mammals. Blackwell. Oxford.

842 **Standen, R.,** 1897.

Some observations by English naturalists on the fauna of Rathlin Island, and Ballycastle district. *Ir. Nat.,* **6**: 173-178. ● Includes analysis of long-eared owl pellets.

843 **Stanley, Lord,** 1833.

(Exhibit of Irish hare). *Trans. Linn. Soc.,* **17**: 555. ● Merely the notice of an exhibit.

844 **Stelfox, A. W.,** 1921.

Curious behaviour of a bat. *Ir. Nat.,* **30**: 109.

845 **Stelfox, A. W.,** 1927.

The grey squirrel spreads to Westmeath. *Ir. Nat. J.,* **1**: 275.

846 **Stelfox, A. W.,** 1965.

Notes on the Irish 'wild cat'. *Ir. Nat. J.,* **15**: 57-60. ● Probably the most objective and conclusive discussion of the subject.

847 ***Stendall, J. A. S.,** 1920.

Rats: their habits and economics. *Proc. Belf. Nat. Fld Club,* (2) **8**: 111-112.

848 **Stendall, J. A. S.,** 1926.
Bottle-nosed whale in Belfast Lough. *Ir. Nat. J.,* **1**: 153.

849 **Stendall, J. A. S.,** 1933.
Badgers at home in Co. Down. *Ir. Nat. J.,* **4**: 218-219. ● Observations at a set.

850 **Stendall, J. A. S.,** 1941.
Pine marten in Co. Londonderry. *Ir. Nat. J.,* **7**: 314.

851 **Stendall, J. A. S.,** 1946.
Pine marten in Ireland. *Ir. Nat. J.,* **8**: 332-333. ● Nineteen records from taxidermist's lists.

852 **Stendall, J. A. S.,** 1947.
Pine marten in Co. Down. *Ir. Nat. J.,* **9**: 48.

853 **Stendall, J. A. S.,** 1948.
A white whale off Co. Clare, Co. Mayo. *Ir. Nat. J.,* **9**: 215.

854 **Stenning, A. N.,** 1895.
Strange capture of otters. *Field,* **86**: 708. ● Otters in eel-nets.

855 **Stewart, J. V.,** 1832.
A list of, and remarks on, some of the mammalious animals, and the birds, met with in the three years preceding December 4, 1828, on the northern coast of Donegal. *Mag. nat. Hist.,* **5**: 578-586.

856 **Stewart, S. A.,** 1883.
Rathlin Island, with notes on its natural history and

antiquities. *Proc. Rep. Belf. nat. Hist. phil. Soc.*, (1882-83): 27-31.

857 **Swiney, J. H. H.,** 1917.
Bat flying in daylight. *Ir. Nat.,* **26**: 36.

858 **Symes, R. G.,** 1874.
The red deer of Erris. *Field,* **44**: 80.

859 **Teacher, D. and Gough, K.,** 1936.
Stoats capturing fish. *Ir. Nat. J.,* **6**: 152.

860 **Tegetmier, W. B.,** 1902.
Supposed hybrid between *Lepus europeus* and *L. variabilis. Field,* **100**: 1074. ● Unusual variation in Irish hare.

861 **Tegner, H.,** 1951.
The Roe Deer. Batchworth. London.

862 ***Tegner, H.,** 1969.
Wild Hares. Baker. London. ● Chapter on the Irish hare.

863 **Templeton, R.,** 1837.
Irish vertebrate animals: selected from the papers of the late John Templeton, Esq. Cranmore. *Mag. nat. Hist.,* (2) **1**: 403-413. ● List of mammals with notes on their abundance.

864 **Thomas, O.,** 1895.
Assogue (*Putorius hibernicus*): a peculiar British mammal. *Nat. Sci.,* **40**: 377-378.

865 *Thomas, O., 1895.
The Irish stoat. *Zoologist*, (3) **19**: 186.

866 Thomas, O. and Barrett-Hamilton, G. E. H., 1895.
The Irish stoat distinct from the British. *Ann. Mag. nat. Hist.*, (6) **15**: 374-375.

867 Thomas, O. and Barrett-Hamilton, G. E. C., 1895.
The Irish stoat distinct from the British species. *Zoologist*, (3) **19**: 124-129.

868 Thompson, D'A. T., 1901.
Risso's dolphin: a cetacean new to the Irish fauna. *Ir. Nat.*, **10**: 88-89.

869 Thompson, G. B., 1935.
The parasites of British birds and mammals IV [V]. Records of mammal parasites. *Entomologist's mon. Mag.*, **71**: 214-219.

870 Thompson, G. B., 1967.
The parasites of British birds and mammals XLVI. Summary of records of *Ixodes* (*Exopalpiger*) *trianguliceps* (Birula, 1895) (Ixodoidea). *Entomologist's Gaz.*, **103**: 146-152. ● From fieldmice.

871 *Thompson, W., 1837.
(Additions to the fauna of Ireland). *Athaneum*, (1837): 468. ● Mention only of *Lepus vermicularis* [?], *Mus hibernicus and Cervus hibernicus* [*giganteus?*]. No detail.

872 Thompson, W., 1837.
Notes, relating chiefly to the natural history of Ireland. *Proc. zool. Soc. Lond.*, (1837): 52-66.

873 **Thompson, W., 1838.**

On the Irish hare (*Lepus hibernicus*). *Trans. R. Ir. Acad.*, **18**: 260-271. ● Very detailed description and other interesting notes.

874 **Thompson, W., 1840.**

Note on the occurrence at various times of the bottle-nosed whale (*Hyperoodon butzkoph*, Lacep.) on the coast of Ireland; and its nearly simultaneous appearance on different parts of the British coast in the autumn of 1839. *Ann. Mag. nat. Hist.*, **4**: 375-381.

875 **Thompson, W., 1840.**

Additions to the fauna of Ireland. *Ann. Mag. nat. Hist.*, **5**: 6-14. ● Whale.

876 **Thompson, W., 1840.**

Report on the fauna of Ireland. Div. Vertebrata. *Rep. Br. Ass. Advmt Sci.*, (Glasgow: 1840): 353-409.

877 **Thompson, W., 1844.**

Additions to the fauna of Ireland. *Ann. Mag. nat. Hist.*, **13**: 430-440. ● Includes a record of a nematode from a dolphin.

878 **Thompson, W., 1844.**

Report on the fauna of Ireland. Div. Invertebrata. *Rep. Br. Ass. Advmt Sci.*, (Cork: 1843): 245-290. ● Includes a list of Irish endoparasites. Hosts are not given. This is the only reference included where mammals are not actually mentioned.

879 **Thompson, W., 1844.**

(Exhibit of Alpine and Irish hares for the purpose of showing that the species are identical). *Rep. Br.*

Ass. Advmt Sci., (Cork: 1843): (Notices and abstracts section) 68.

880 **Thompson, W., 1846.**
Notice of a bottle-nosed whale *Hyperoodon butzkoph,* Lancep., obtained in Belfast Bay in October, 1845. *Ann. Mag. nat. Hist.,* **17**: 150-153.

881 **Thompson, W., 1846.**
Additions to the fauna of Ireland, including species new to that of Britain;—with notes on rare species. *Ann. Mag. nat. Hist.,* **18**: 310-315. ● Only mammal a whale.

882 **Thompson, W., 1849-56.**
The Natural History of Ireland. Bohn. London. ● By far the most authoritative text at the time. Besides the section on mammals, there are notes on the mammalian prey of several raptorial birds.

883 ***Thorburn, A., 1920.**
British Mammals. Longmans, Green. London. ● Little on Irish mammals.

884 **'.303', 1902.**
Weight of fallow deer. *Field,* **100**: 681.

885 **T. J. D., 1895.**
Badgers in County Kerry. *Field,* **86**: 172.

886 **Tomes, T. P., 1896.**
Hare running to earth. *Field,* **87**: 139.

887 **Turk, F. A., 1945.**
Studies of Acari 5. Notes on and descriptions of new

and little known British Acari. *Ann. Mag. nat. Hist.,* (11) **12**: 785-820. ● Material from fieldmouse included.

888 **Turk, F. A. and Turk, S. M., 1952.**
Studies of Acari 7th series: Records and descriptions of mites new to the British fauna, together with short notes on sundry species. *Ann. Mag. nat. Hist.,* (12) **5**: 475-506. ● Material from fieldmouse included.

889 **Twamley, W. M., 1892.**
Hare encumbered with balls of snow. *Field,* **79**: 432. ● Heresay. See also page 508 for possible explanation.

890 **Tyrrell, W. J. H., 1889.**
Leverets in February. *Field,* **73**: 260.

891 **'Upper Ormond', 1893.**
The squirrel in Ireland. *Field,* **82**: 791.

892 **Ussher, R. J., 1882.**
Notes on the Irish red deer. *Zoologist,* (3) **6**: 81-84.

893 **Ussher, R. J., 1883.**
Vermin destroyed on an Irish estate. *Zoologist,* (3) **7**: 171-172. ● List.

894 **Ussher, R. J., 1886.**
Bird life on the Saltees and the Keraghs, Co. Wexford. *Zoologist* (3) **10**: 88-98. ● Rabbit and hedgehog remains at peregrine's plucking place.

895 **Ussher, R. J., 1898.**
Breeding of the marten in Co. Waterford. *Ir. Nat.,* **7**: 171-172.

896 **Ussher, R. J., 1908.**
Supposed occurrence of a wild cat in the west of Cork. *Ir. Nat.,* **17**: 140-141.

897 **Ussher, R. J., 1911.**
Badgers in Ireland. *Field,* **117**: 649.

898 **Ussher, R. J. and Warren, R., 1900.**
The Birds of Ireland. Gurney and Jackson. London. ● Includes records of mammals as food of raptorial birds.

899 **Various authors, 1874.**
Natural history of Ireland. *Field,* **43**: 264, 272, 297, 347, 430, 445, 469, 524. ● Notes and correspondence on local faunas with many references to mammals.

900 **Various authors, 1892.**
The badger in Ireland. *Field,* **80**: 707, 726, 764. ● Correspondence on badgers from several localities. Includes note on badgers as food.

901 **Venables, U. M. and Venables, L. S. V., 1960.**
A seal survey of Northern Ireland. *Proc. zool. Soc. Lond.,* **133**: 490-494.

902 **Walker, J. and Fairley, J. S., 1968.**
Food of Irish hares in Co. Antrim, Ireland. *J. Mammal.,* **49**: 783-785. ● Analyses of stomach contents.

903 **Wallace, A. R.,** 1892.

Island Life. McMillan. London. (Second edition). ●
Brief mention of the origin of the Irish mammal
fauna.

904 **Wallis, H. M.,** 1877.

Marten-cat in Scotland and Ireland. *Zoologist,* (3) **1:**
292.

905 **Walton, G. A.,** 1965.

Pastureland infestation by the sheep tick (*Ixodes
ricinus* L.) as indicated by parasitism of the brown
rat (*Rattus norvegicus* Berk.). *J. med. Ent.,* **1:** 326-
328.

906 **Walton, G. A.,** 1967.

A site of particular zoological interest—Doughruagh
Mountain, Kylemore, Co. Galway. *Ir. Nat. J.,* **15:** 309-
312. ● Includes a record of a pine marten.

907 **Walton, G. A.,** 1967.

Relative status in Britain and Ireland of louping-ill
encephalitis virus. *J. med. Ent.,* **4:** 161-167. ● Ticks
on rodents.

908 **Walton, G. A. and O'Donnell, T. G.,** 1969.

Observations on *Ixodes ricinus* and louping-ill virus
in Ireland. *Proc. int. Congr. Acarology,* **2:** 601-608.
● Occurrence on wild mammals and distribution.

909 **Ward, R.,** 1911.

Pine marten in Co. Kerry. *Field,* **118:** 1350.

910 **Warrand, R. E.,** 1895.

Irish hare turning white in winter. *Zoologist,* (3) **19:**
104-105.

911 **Warren, R., 1880.**
Grey seal in Killala Bay, Co. Mayo. *Zoolog'st,* (3) **4**: 358-359.

912 **Warren, R., 1885.**
Is the weasel a native of Ireland? *Field,* **66**: 671.

913 **Warren, R., 1886.**
Destruction of young rabbits by rats. *Zoologist,* (3) **10**: 241-242.

914 **Warren, R. 1893.**
Occurrence of the hump-backed whale off Sligo. *Field,* **81**: 535-536.

915 **Warren, R., 1893.**
The hump-backed whale on the Irish coast. *Ir. Nat.,* **2**: 119-120.

916 **Warren, R., 1893.**
Hump-backed whale on the coast of Sligo. *Zoologist,* (3) **17**: 188-189.

917 **Warren, R., 1905.**
Supposed wild cat in Ireland. *Ir. Nat.,* **14**: 135-136.

918 **Warren, R., 1905.**
Wild cat formerly indiginous in Ireland. *Ir. Nat.,* **14**: 166.

919 **Warren, R., 1905.**
The wild cat in Ireland. *Ir. Nat.,* **14**: 183-184.

920 **Warren, R., 1905.**
Seals in Killala Bay and the Moy Estuary, Co. Mayo. *Zoologist,* (4) **9**: 134-139.

921 **Warren, R.,** 1907.

Is the weasel a native of Ireland? *Zoologist,* (4) **11**: 29.

922 **Warren, R.,** 1907.

Dolphin in Moy Estuary, Killala Bay. *Zoologist,* (4) **11**: 235.

923 **Warren, R.,** 1911.

Wild cat supposed to be within historic times a native of Ireland. *Ir. Nat.,* **20**: 80, 96.

924 **Warwick, T.,** 1934.

The distribution of the muskrat (*Fiber zibethicus*) in the British Isles. *J. Anim. Ecol.,* **3**: 250-267.

925 **Warwick, T.,** 1940.

A contribution to the ecology of the musk-rat (*Ondatra zibethica*) in the British Isles. *Proc. zool. Soc. Lond.,* **110**: 165-201. ● A few new facts from Ireland.

926 **Watt, H. B.,** 1923.

The American grey squirrel in Ireland. *Ir. Nat.,* **32**: 95.

927 **W. C. H.,** 1916.

The Isles of Arran. *Field,* **128**: 7. ● Rats, rabbits and fieldmice recorded.

928 **Webb, A.,** 1876.

Hedgehogs in Ireland. *Zoologist,* (2) **11**: 4824-4825. ● Includes weights of young reared in captivity.

929 **Welch, R. J.,** 1905.

The last wild red deer, Co. Donegal. *Ir. Nat.,* **14**: 120.

930 **Welch, R. J.,** 1929.
Porpoises and seals in Strangford Lough. *Ir. Nat. J.,* **2**: 245.

931 **Welch, R. J.,** 1933-34.
A porpoise in a Co. Armagh river. *Ir. Nat. J.,* **4**: 154; **5**: 96. ● Not a genuine record.

932 **Weldon, E. F.,** 1881.
Food of the otter. *Field,* **57**: 217. ● Otter attacks cormorant.

933 **Welland, J.,** 1898.
The whiskered bat in Co. Dublin. *Ir. Nat.,* **7**: 272.

934 **West, Newman and Co.,** 1913.
Marten in Co. Mayo. *Field,* **122**: 666.

935 **'West of Ireland',** 1858.
Red deer in Ireland. *Field,* **14**: 282. ● Last red deer in Co. Mayo. Comments by other anonymous writers appended.

936 **W. H. A.,** 1894.
Stoats climbing trees. *Field,* **83**: 169.

937 **Whitehead, G. K.,** 1950.
Deer and their Management in the Deer Parks of Great Britain and Ireland. Country Life. London.

938 **Whitehead, G. K.,** 1960.
The Deer Stalking Grounds of Great Britain and Ireland. Hollis and Carter. London.

939 **Whitehead, G. K.,** 1964.
The Deer of Great Britain and Ireland. Routledge and Kegan Paul. London. ● A comprehensive account.

940 **Whitty, B. T.,** 1955.
Myxomatosis in the common hare—*Lepus europaeus* —I. *Ir. vet. J.,* **9**: 267-268. ● Hare with myxomatosis (*L. europaeus?*). See also No. 186.

941 **Whyte, J. J.,** 1874.
Weasels in Ireland. *Field,* **44**: 31. ● Supposed record.

942 **Whyte, J. J.,** 1874.
The Irish hare turning white in winter. *Field,* **44**: 87.

943 **Whyte, J. J.,** 1876.
Colour of Irish hares. *Field,* **47**: 158. ● White hares.

944 **Whyte, J. J.,** 1876.
The marten in the west of Ireland. *Field,* **47**: 638.

945 **Wilde, W.,** 1859.
Upon the unmanufactured animal remains belonging to the Academy. *Proc. R. Ir. Acad.,* **7**: 181-211. ● General. Includes records of martens.

946 **Williams, A.,** 1882.
Variety of the Irish hare. *Zoologist,* (3) **6**: 66-67.

947 **Williams and Son,** 1878.
Black hare in Ireland. *Zoologist,* (3) **2**: 434.

948 **Williams, E.,** 1890.
Varieties of the hare in Ireland. *Zoologist,* (3) **14:** 70-71.

949 **Williams, R. P.,** 1858, 1860.
(On a black and white variety of field mouse). *Proc. Dubl. nat. Hist. Soc.,* (1860) **2:** 104. Also in *Nat. Hist. Rev.,* (Proceedings of the Societies section) (1858) **5:** 188.

950 **Williams, W.,** 1874.
Irish hare turning white in winter. *Field,* **44:** 81.

951 **Williams, W. J.,** 1916.
Absence of the polecat from Ireland. *Field,* **127:** 848.
● See No. 38.

952 **Wilson, J. M.,** 1911.
Badger in Co. Longford. *Field,* **117:** 537.

953 **Wood-Martin, W. G.,** 1892.
History of Sligo, County and Town. Book VIII. Hodges and Figgis. Dublin. ● Notes on the local mammals.

954 **Workman, W. H.,** 1902.
Golden eagle in Co. Donegal. *Zoologist,* (4) **6:** 150.
● Heresay reference to eagles killing hares.

955 **Workman, W. H.,** 1926.
The wolf (*Canis lupus*) in Ireland. *Ir. Nat. J.,* **1:** 43-44. ● Some early records.

956 **Workman, W. H.,** 1926.
A tame hedgehog. *Ir. Nat. J.,* **1:** 83.

957 **Wright, C. E.,** 1909.
Helix nemoralis eaten by rabbits. *J. Conch., Lond.,* **12**: 268.

Wright, T., 1892. See No. 355.

958 **W. W. W.,** 1882.
Marten in Co. Galway. *Field,* **59**: 887.

959 **Yarrell, W.,** 1833.
Characters of the Irish hare, a new species of the genus *Lepus,* Linn. *Proc. zool. Soc. Lond.,* (1833): 88.

960 **Young, A.,** 1780.
A Tour of Ireland with General Observations on the State of the Kingdom. Bonham. Dublin. ● Includes notes on a Donegal whale-fishery and a brief reference to rabbits.

961 **Young, T. A.,** 1885.
Agility of the otter. *Field,* **65**: 21. ● Otter takes moorhen.

962 **Young, W.,** 1900.
Rorqual or finwhale on the coast of Galway. *Field,* **95**: 859. ● Stranding.

963 **Z,** 1870.
Irish and variable hares. *Field,* **36**: 236. ● No difference in size between Irish and variable hares.

INDEX

It will be seen below that, although some species are entered individually, several have been dealt with collectively in higher taxa. In some cases this seemed more appropriate, not only because a particular group as a whole was of more interest, but also because in some publications the species were not clearly defined: for example in the case of hares. All the references given against a particular taxon deal substantially with it. Exceptionally—where a reference is not primarily concerned with Irish mammals—the relevant sections, which may be relatively brief, pertain to the taxon.

It should be noted that wolves have been extinct in Ireland for some two hundred years, and that there is no conclusive evidence that weasels and wild cats ever existed there. The Irish stoat is smaller than that in Great Britain and is commonly known as 'the weasel', which no doubt accounts for the supposed occurrences of the latter species. Alleged specimens of wild cat have, when examined, invariably proved to be feral examples of the domestic cat.

Order Insectivora

Erinaceus europaeus Hedgehog

51	210	239	356	541	581	586	598	638	686	705	719
743	823	894	928	956							

Sorex minutus Pigmy shrew

5	7	150	154	171	190	201	256	462	588	599

Order Chiroptera

Bats

9	10	11	12	13	14	18	19	80	87	94	97
98	102	103	104	112	114	122	156	157	158	159	182
206	234	302	305	316	318	319	327	329	342	349	351
376	384	387	397	400	406	448	451	452	453	454	459

463	467	471	473	478	481	482	483	484	485	486	491
498	500	517	518	520	540	563	579	582	583	585	586
587	589	590	591	592	594	595	613	614	615	616	617
625	639	644	645	646	647	651	652	653	654	655	658
684	687	691	692	693	703	712	715	716	721	722	729
741	765	766	768	770	771	772	786	811	826	844	857
933											

Order Lagomorpha

Lepus species Hares

17	40	42	65	73	74	75	76	79	81	83	85
92	165	175	177	179	185	186	193	208	215	218	226
227	247	306	307	308	326	383	428	431	457	470	480
493	503	507	508	512	530	561	572	606	609	621	626
631	632	657	661	689	697	747	754	778	782	827	843
860	862	871	873	879	886	889	890	902	910	940	942
943	946	947	948	950	954	959	963				

Oryctolagus cuniculus Rabbit

| 6 | 71 | 101 | 109 | 115 | 145 | 185 | 210 | 218 | 219 | 229 | 235 |
| 242 | 248 | 322 | 375 | 607 | 677 | 733 | 894 | 913 | 957 | 960 | |

Order Rodentia

Apodemus sylvaticus Fieldmouse

44	82	111	132	166	169	172	181	187	190	240	249
250	251	252	253	255	256	263	264	265	266	281	283
285	294	297	384	385	419	423	429	463	464	468	539
611	674	678	701	704	828	870	887	888	949		

Clethrionomys glareolus Bank vole

| 168 | 269 | 279 | 286 | 288 | 291 | 292 | 300 | 643 |

Mus musculus House mouse

| 105 | 181 | 190 | 287 | 422 | 455 | 539 | 612 | 664 | 665 | 666 |

Rattus species Rats

46	59	61	68	100	106	109	130	131	136	144	173
174	194	216	303	344	374	405	510	519	556	557	558
608	610	623	690	696	702	705	756	769	840	847	871
905	913										

Sciurus carolinensis Grey squirrel

340	341	420	447	565	566	567	568	820	821	822	845
926											

Sciurus vulgaris Red squirrel

1	43	60	67	70	110	118	198	230	233	240	245
416	460	499	501	506	515	521	531	564	565	584	593
596	597	605	630	637	740	757	764	806	808	819	820
822	836	891									

Order Carnivora

Canis lupus Wolf

15	189	309	372	402	421	475	504	516	545	546	549
628	807	809	814	815	955						

Felis species Wild cat

91	117	388	389	417	474	493	559	787	789	797	798
846	896	917	918	919	923						

Lutra lutra Otter

32	50	67	89	182	199	207	231	241	244	310	331
352	371	377	396	408	418	430	434	437	438	439	440
442	470	480	502	513	532	543	544	559	603	619	662
792	801	812	824	825	854	932	961				

Martes martes Pine marten

86	96	116	119	120	148	163	180	195	203	205	217
238	246	278	312	313	314	315	321	346	350	353	362

380	381	382	393	398	401	407	409	410	435	441	445
472	477	490	522	536	560	562	573	575	577	578	602
627	683	694	710	711	713	714	720	736	745	758	760
763	767	815	850	851	852	895	904	906	909	934	944
945	958										

Meles meles Badger

| 33 | 52 | 99 | 149 | 262 | 311 | 328 | 353 | 364 | 436 | 446 | 465 |
| 476 | 480 | 600 | 633 | 735 | 737 | 743 | 849 | 885 | 897 | 900 | 952 |

Mustela erminea hibernica Irish stoat

88	178	196	199	204	212	222	229	243	289	444	487
480	497	514	533	572	576	601	695	733	742	793	859
864	865	866	867	936							

Mustela nivalis Weasel

| 134 | 196 | 237 | 411 | 444 | 456 | 494 | 656 | 912 | 921 | 941 |

Pinnipedia Seals

34	41	49	162	209	223	331	343	354	359	424	425
426	524	525	526	527	528	529	547	553	634	641	744
759	795	796	805	835	901	911	920	930			

Vulpes vulpes Fox

149	191	192	214	243	254	259	261	267	268	270	271
272	273	274	275	276	282	284	290	293	328	330	357
363	443	466	538	604	675	717	718	749	755	761	779

Order Artiodactyla

Cervidae Deer

54	135	139	140	141	160	200	211	224	225	280	310
322	345	392	404	413	475	496	505	537	559	569	622
628	629	642	649	688	698	699	700	734	746	748	750
803	815	837	838	858	861	884	892	929	935	937	938
939											

Order Cetacea

Whales

20	21	22	23	24	25	26	27	29	30	31	35
36	37	39	58	62	63	64	66	69	77	78	84
128	146	147	151	152	153	155	161	184	197	202	213
232	296	304	332	333	334	335	336	337	338	339	358
359	360	361	365	366	367	368	369	370	373	378	379
386	390	391	394	395	399	427	449	450	458	495	509
511	523	547	552	620	624	659	682	707	709	726	727
728	730	731	732	739	753	784	785	788	794	800	802
804	813	814	816	839	848	853	868	874	875	877	880
881	914	915	916	922	930	931	960	962			

Other species

4	38	113	120	137	220	221	348	412	494	781	924
925	951										

The above list is by no means exhaustive. Some of the entries against one species may, in addition, deal comparatively briefly with others. For example, a paper on the food of a carnivore might well describe mammalian prey. Papers of a broader nature were excluded (dealing with several species): those on general topics, local mammal faunas, food of raptorial birds and collections of parasites from a range of mammalian hosts. The section of the index below has therefore been compiled to facilitate a more exhaustive search. For the sake of completeness all references pertinent to the various headings are included.

Early references

(before 1820)

47	133	355	479	547	628	640	774	775	832	833	834
960											

General

2	3	8	47	53	72	90	95	121	123	126	133
176	183	187	188	220	228	317	323	324	325	326	355
403	461	469	479	489	535	542	548	570	572	574	580
609	618	650	685	723	734	751	752	774	776	777	780
783	790	799	815	841	872	876	882	883	893	903	945

Local mammal faunas

16	48	107	108	124	125	138	164	190	200	320	414
415	433	483	492	547	548	550	551	571	635	640	660
724	725	738	751	774	775	791	832	833	834	855	863
899	953										

Mammals on off-shore islands

28	55	56	57	71	93	142	143	150	154	171	183
236	252	253	347	473	534	554	555	556	648	663	665
679	681	706	708	817	818	856	894	927			

Mammals as food of avian predators

4	145	219	257	258	260	295	298	299	301	375	571
723	773	811	827	842	882	894	898	954			

Mammals as food of mammalian predators

210	243	254	259	261	262	284	289	600	601	733	913

Parasites, epifauna and disease

40	45	103	125	127	129	156	157	158	166	167	169
170	172	186	190	191	192	218	236	249	250	251	252
253	255	276	277	279	285	286	289	340	341	342	344
384	385	432	436	478	538	539	563	636	644	645	651
653	654	667	668	669	670	671	672	673	674	675	676
677	678	679	680	681	684	701	703	762	828	829	830
831	837	869	870	877	878	887	888	905	907	908	940

ADDENDA

Since compiling this reference list the following relevant papers have been published.

Fairley, J. S., 1972.

Food of otters from Co. Galway, Ireland, and notes on other aspects of their biology. *J. Zool., Lond.,* 166: 469-474. ● Includes dimensions, reproduction, parasites.

Fairley, J. S. and Clark, F. L., 1972.

Further records of fleas from Irish birds and mammals. *Entomologists' Gaz.,* 23: 66-68.

Fairley, J. S. and Clark, F. L., 1972.

Notes on pipistrelle bats *Pipistrellus pipistrellus* Schreber from a colony in Co. Galway. *Ir. Nat. J.,* 17: 190-193. ● Dimensions, reproduction, parasites.

Fairley, J. S. and Clark, F. L., 1972.

Food of barn owls *Tyto alba* (Scopoli) over one year at a roost in Co. Galway. *Ir. Nat. J.,* 17: 219-222. ● From analyses of pellets.

Fairley, J. S. and Wilson, S. C., 1972.

Autumn food of otters on the Agivey River, Co. Londonderry, Northern Ireland. *J. Zool., Lond.,* 166: 468-469. ● From spraint analysis.

Lang, J. T., 1972.

Risso's dolphin (*Grampus griseus*) in Co. Mayo. *Ir. Nat. J.,* 17: 246.

Mulloy, F., 1972.

Japanese sika deer (*Cervus nippon nippon*). *Ir. Nat. J.,* **17**: 246.